FRIEND *or* FRENEMY?

ALSO BY ANDREA LAVINTHAL AND JESSICA ROZLER

The Hookup Handbook:
A Single Girl's Guide to Living It Up

Erin Fitzsimmons

ABOUT THE AUTHORS

ANDREA LAVINTHAL (right) is an editor at *Cosmopolitan*. Her likes: dessert, a white wine spritzer on a warm summer night (seriously), and watching *Gossip Girl*. She lives, works, shops, and lives to shop in New York City.

JESSICA ROZLER works in book publishing. Her likes: comfort foods, a tall pint of Guinness on a cold winter night, and reruns of *The Golden Girls*. She lives, works, plays, and lives to play in New York City.

FRIEND *or* FRENEMY?

A Guide to the Friends You Need

and the Ones You Don't

Andrea Lavinthal and Jessica Rozler

HARPER

NEW YORK • LONDON • TORONTO • SYDNEY

HARPER

HarperCollins books may be purchased for educational, business, or sales promotional use. For information please write: Special Markets Department, HarperCollins Publishers, 10 East 53rd Street, New York, NY 10022.

FIRST EDITION

Designed by Joy O'Meara
Illustrations by Michael Ahern

Library of Congress Cataloging-in-Publication Data is available upon request.

ISBN 978-0-06-156203-7

08 09 10 11 12 OV/RRD 10 9 8 7 6 5 4 3 2 1

To our friends, our second family

ACKNOWLEDGMENTS

Before we get this show on the road, we first want to thank all of the people who made *Friend or Frenemy?* possible. Heaps of gratitude to the entire team at Harper, including: Jeanette Perez, our wonderful editor; Audrey Harris, Alberto Rojas, and Caroline Sun, our publicists; Mary Beth Constant, production editor; Robin Bilardello, who created a great cover; and Michael Ahern, for the fabulous illustrations.

We're also forever grateful to our tireless and fearless agent, Adam Chromy of Artists and Artisans Inc. You've been with us from the beginning, and your energy and enthusiasm are contagious. Thank you, thank you.

We're also very grateful to John Searles at *Cosmopolitan* for his encouragement. Also, a big thank you to our families for all of their love and support.

And, last, but certainly not least, a mega-huge, supersized thanks to all of our great friends. We're lucky to have you. You've been there through thick and thin, boot-cut and straight leg, headache and heartbreak. You are the polar opposite of frenemies.

CONTENTS

introduction
You Get By with a Little Help from Your Friends xv

Part One
Friendly Conversation 1

chapter one
The Friend Commandments 3

chapter two
Through the Years: A Timelime of Semi-recent Triumphs and Tragedies in Girlfriend History 9

chapter three
Textual Healing: The New Rules of Digital Engagement 15

Part Two
Your Buddy List: The People in Your Social Stratosphere 45

chapter four
We Are Framily: Your Closest Confidantes 47

chapter five
The Daily Grind: Cubicle Comrades, Worker Bee-otches, and the Other People All Up in Your Office Space 69

chapter six
Frenemies: The Users, Losers, and Abusers
Who You Need to De-MySpace Right Now 91

chapter seven
Like Kissing Your Brother: Boy Friends 117

chapter eight
Because Like Paula Abdul Said, Opposites Attract:
Your Unlikely Friendships 137

chapter nine
Outerspace: Lunch Dates, Drinking Buddies,
and Various Other Acquaintances 149

Part Three
That's What Friends Are (and Aren't) For 163

chapter ten
Balancing Friendship and Coupledom 165

chapter eleven
Threesomes (And Get Your Head Out of the Gutter
Because We're Not Talking *Those* Kinds of Threesomes):
Navigating the Sometimes Murky Waters of a Friendship Trio 183

chapter twelve
When the Friendship Sinks: Breaking Up,
Making Up, and Moving On 191

chapter thirteen
Misery Loves Company:
The Challenges of Making New Friends 211

chapter fourteen
Everything You Need to Know About Friendship You Learned in Kindergarten—Right? 225

in closing
Why Friends Are Just as Important as Boyfriends 229

introduction

• • • • • • • • • •

YOU GET BY WITH A LITTLE HELP FROM YOUR FRIENDS

There was a time, a simpler time, when turning sweet sixteen meant keys to your mom's old Buick instead of keys to a brand-new Beemer, McDreamy was just a frozen dessert at McDonald's, and a few things were certain: George Michael was straight, starlets kept their privates *private* (unless, of course, they were making a very "artistic" film), and, most important, you knew exactly who your friends were.

These days, nothing is quite the same. George got caught one-handed in a public bathroom; a bevy of actresses got very publicly exposed as they exited Escalades, danced at nightclubs, walked down the street—you name it; and you've got yourself 1,214 friends on Facebook, five of whom you've actually met in person.

In this era of e-mating and relating, of instant communication, gratification, and *get*ification, the rules of conduct—especially when it comes to friendship—are changing. Socializing via cyberspace is no longer reserved for thirteen-year-old Fall Out Boy fans and forty-eight-year-old fans of thirteen-year-old boys. Now, with the click of a mouse, you can befriend and break up, hook up and make up all without ever having to leave the warm glow of your computer screen and do something unthinkable like interact with a real, live human being.

Even if online social networking isn't exactly your cup of Tazo, you can't deny the obvious: cell phones, CrackBerries, and various other shiny things that ring and ding have increased the *quantity* of our communication and not always the *quality*. This express checkout way of life can help make connections with new people, but it can also limit how meaningful those relationships can be—much in the same way that you have twenty pairs of jeans in your closet and only two that you actually wear.

Before we get too carried away, though, you should know that this book isn't about the evils of the Internet. After all, we're part of the iPod, Netflix, and e-everything generation, not some crusty old technophobes who read *Reader's Digest* by candlelight and gripe about gosh-darned kids today and their newfangled electronic gadgets. We believe e-mail and the aforementioned shiny things that ring and ding can make it a lot easier to stay in touch with people. They also add some much-needed convenience to our busy lives. The problem is that sometimes too much of a good thing can actually be pretty bad. (Think: Botox and self-tanner.) In other words, you can power-walk through your day with an iPhone attached to your ear, but that will never replace good old-fashioned face-to-face interaction with people.

It all sounds simple enough, right? When it comes to friendships, you get what you give and have to get away from your computer if you want to make real-life connections. Well, someone isn't getting the message. Even though we have more ways to stay in contact with one another than ever, according to a semi-recent study from Duke University, Americans today have fewer confidantes than they did back in the mid-eighties, a time when cell phones were scarce and friends let friends have Flock of Seagulls hair. The study also revealed that more and more people admit that they have no one they can confide in at all.

We find this tidbit of information rather troubling, because no man is an island (nor can one man carry a movie about an island, as we learned from *Cast Away*). We need to be part of a network of friends, a community of people with different strengths, weaknesses, backgrounds, and personalities.

Going back to what we were saying before, this book isn't about the evils of technology. Rather, it's a look at the modern state of our comrades and confidantes during a time of friendship crisis—a time when we are more connected to the rest of the world than ever, yet increasingly detached from one another. This book is also an honest look at the rules and etiquette of friendship, covering everything from becoming a better friend and adding new people to your social circle to dealing with frenemies and surviving friendship breakups.

Simply put, we think it's time that friends get their due. You see, every day we are bombarded with helpful "advice" about how to snag a guy and hypnotize him using some sort of *Cosmo Kama Sutra* booty voodoo, but no one ever really talks about the other important relationships in a woman's life: those she has with her pals, her confidantes, her girls. Thanks to our constant education in the arena of manhandling, we all know what we're supposed to do when a guy stops calling (duh—drive past his house every hour on the hour with our headlights off), but what happens when your BFF stops returning your calls or you are forced to play Switzerland in the middle to two feuding friends?

Everything is changing right now—especially in your twenties and thirties. Some people get married, others have kids, and others are single. Some never leave their hometowns, while others join the Peace Corps and travel to faraway lands, even though you know they will burst out crying as soon as they see a "poor person" and go running back to the comfort of Mom and Dad's McMansion, which is situated in a cozy cul-de-sac.

Finding common ground is no longer as easy as walking down the block to your best friend's house (which just happened to have had the biggest, raddest swimming pool in the neighborhood). It requires a lot more effort to stay in touch with your friends and keep those relationships alive than it used to. Think of friend maintenance like eyebrow maintenance, only in reverse: You need to put in the effort to keep from growing apart. Of course, it's worth it because no one wants to be alone or have a unibrow.

Below, we present more reasons why friendship is changing, seasoned with a dash of why we need our friends more than ever.

Additional Reasons Why the Face of Friendship Is Changing

Reason #1: We ain't gettin' any younger. (Except for Demi Moore. Bitch doesn't age.)

Despite slathering on rejuvenating eye cream, bending and twisting our bodies in classes like yogalates and cardio-roller-strip-ballet, and watching shows on MTV that are geared toward a twelve- to twelve-and-a-half-year-old demographic, none of us are actually getting any younger. As we progress ever so gracefully beyond young adulthood, our social networks are expanding like crazy. Gone are the days when your crew consisted of your best friend, Ally, who conveniently lived next door to you and had the coolest L.A. Gear high-tops, your hamster Boo-Boo Bear, and your imaginary friend, Princess Buttercup. Times changed and so did you. Ally eventually grew up and got knocked up, Boo-Boo Bear chewed through an electrical cord in your parents' living room and got zapped into that big hamster wheel in the sky, and the Princess became a memory after your mom accidentally sat on her. (May she rest in peace.)

As we get older and our number of responsibilities increases, we have more opportunities to make friends. Suddenly, we have work buddies, childhood pals, college friends, our significant other's friends—the list goes on and on. On the other hand, as we grow older, our tolerance for B.S. dwindles. We are more likely to hold our true-blue buds close and finally have the courage to leave the ditchers in our dust. (You know this particular brand of frenemy. She's the one who sticks to you like glue when she's single and then flees the scene faster than one of the pervs on *Dateline*'s "To Catch a Predator" as soon as a new guy comes around. More about her later in the book.)

Reason #2: We have a major case of life attention deficit disorder.

We are Generation Y Settle, and moving from city to city and job to job is the way we operate. Today, we also have what our parents and grandparents did not: choices. Hell, you could say that we have an Old Country Buffet of opportunity. When the going gets tough (re: boring), we can pull up the stakes and move onward, whether it's to a new career, better digs, or Europe for a few months to hang out with other Americans, pretend to be cultured, and then come back to New Jersey with a Madonna accent.

Regardless of what cutting-edge publications like *Newsweek* and *Time* say about the "boomerang" generation and "kidults" who return home after college to live in their parents' basement and eat food out of their fridge, the truth is that our love of the transient lifestyle makes us more likely to forge out on our own, away from the people who share our genes and closer to the ones with whom we are likely to share our jeans. That leaves our friends to take on a familial role, and, come to think of it, our friends are a lot like our families, minus Nana and her flatulence problem and Grandpa and his penchant for Crown Royal on days that end in *y*.

Reason #3: We're just sooooo busy.

Way back in the day, the only people who needed to be reached 24/7 were doctors and drugs dealers. It wouldn't be uncommon for one of these professionals to be beeped away from a Friday night dinner out with friends to go take care of business, whether it was delivering a baby or a couple of dime bags.

Today, we are all like doctors and drug dealers in the sense that we are reachable all day, everyday. Does your neurotic, bipolar boss need you to swing by the office on a Saturday morning and rub her shoulders, pick out the brown M&Ms from the candy dish on her desk, and reassure her that no, it really is much better to be feared and respected than liked? Now she can easily reach you by cell phone or, better yet, your company-provided CrackBerry!

As we mentioned earlier, our list of responsibilities, both real (working at our jobs) and imagined (wasting time at work by updating our Facebook profiles) is growing. We all have to make an extra effort to stay in touch with those closest to us. Speaking of—let's do lunch. Call us! Kiss-kiss!

To sum it all up, even though our lives, friendships, and means for staying connected to the world are changing, one thing remains the same: our friends are still incredibly important to us. That being said, we would like to welcome you to *Friend or Frenemy?*. We hope you find it to be a funny-because-it's-true and funny-because-it's-actually-funny examination of the contemporary state of friendship. It is also a celebration of great friends, those wonderful people who have been with you through it all—the breakups and breakdowns and the highs and lows. Perhaps *Friend or Frenemy?* will even inspire you to get in touch with an old pal or at least Google-stalk her from the safety and anonymity of the Internet.

Also, there's some other research about friendship that is a bit more enlightening than the aforementioned Duke study, which found that we have fewer friends now than we did back when Bill Cosby sweaters were all the rage: our friends help us live healthier, happier, and longer lives. Of course, we don't need science to tell us that our pals make everything better, but somewhere between *Chicken Soup for the Soul* and *Mean Girls* lies the truth: yes, our friends are beyond important to us, but not everything is always sunshine, teddy bears, and episodes of *Oprah* where she gives everyone in the studio audience a free trip to Canyon Ranch or a Hyundai or a European principality.

We want you to think of *Friend or Frenemy?* as cautiously optimistic and not unlike Katie Couric's CBS newscast: a little helping of icky realism, but in the end, filled with enough footage of water-skiing squirrels and otters holding hands to make you walk away from the experience knowing that everything in the world is going to be okay. And when you think about it, it's kind of like that with our friends. Sometimes we may bicker and make one another wear hideous bridesmaid dresses, but even during the tough moments when we think our world is going to come crashing down, one thing is for sure: your friends are the family you choose.

Now, before we move on to the meat of the book (or the tofu for you vegetarians), let's debunk some myths about friendship.

Common Friendship Myths

MYTH: A friend is a forever thing.

THE TRUTH: There are a few things in this life that are guaranteed to last for all eternity: cockroaches, herpes, and *Saturday Night Live*. Everything else is a crapshoot, and that includes friendship, or any other relationship, for that matter.

Case in point: Let's go back to Ally, your childhood best friend forever. When you were eleven years old, you exchanged best friend necklaces. The two of you had a plan: You would marry the Matthews brothers, live next door to each other in pretty little houses that had great big in-ground swimming pools, and live happily ever. (Of course, when it came to the marriage situation, you would let Ally have Josh Matthews and you would take Chris even though he had a lazy eye, because that was the type of friend you were. Not that it really mattered, anyway, because this was a preadolescent fantasy and the boys were merely minor characters in the lives of you and your best friend.) Then, you and Ally grew older and reality set in. You discovered poetry and Ally got her first real boyfriend (a senior with a mustache and a Mustang), and the two of you eventually drifted apart, down your own life paths. (Last you heard, Ally was happily married to mustache dude and had three kids. You, on the other hand, can't even keep a houseplant alive.)

The dirty little secret is that sometimes friends just drift in different directions and no longer have anything in common. This isn't to say that the oldies aren't goodies, but, when it gets to the point that you see each other only when someone dies, it's probably time to take her off your Christmas card list.

MYTH: *Sex and the City* was a reality show.

THE TRUTH: Perhaps you have crazy curly hair and a best friend, who—how do we put this delicately?—is as easy as the *Star* magazine crossword puzzle. And you might even know a cynical redhead and a WASPy princess who thinks Connecticut is the ultimate aphrodisiac. However, you and your friends are not Carrie, Miranda, Samantha, and Charlotte. Why not? Because they don't exist. Anyway, can't we talk about another show? What about *Arrested Development*?

MYTH: *Will and Grace* was also a reality show.

THE TRUTH: This girl-who-loves-boy-who-loves-boys scenario works well when both parties are single and have lots of time to shop, brunch, and watch *Project Runway* together. However, once the girl gets married and/or the guy starts dating a famous closeted actor, the friendship loses its luster faster than a necklace from the Joan Rivers jewelry collection.

MYTH: Men and women can't just be friends.

THE TRUTH: While we're on the topic of TV, here's something else to think about: Just because many television shows use the Rachel-Ross subplot to keep viewers guessing "will they or won't they" all season long until the gorgeous girl and her lovably dopey best guy pal who could never get someone like her in real life finally share a "shocking" kiss just in time for May sweeps, doesn't mean that men and women can't stay platonic. Life isn't a sitcom, and guys and girls are more than capable of hanging out sans booty. And before you and your Dawson make a pact to marry each other if you both happen to be single when you turn some seemingly old and scary age, keep in mind that thirty is the new twenty, forty is the new thirty, fifty is the new forty, and you need to turn off the TV and get a new hobby. (Just a note: Although *Friend or Frenemy?* mostly focuses on your girls, we never forget that men and women can and should be friends. For more on the men in your life, check out Chapter Seven, "Like Kissing Your Brother: Boy Friends.")

MYTH: Only a boy can break your heart.

THE TRUTH: When you start dating someone, there's always a chance that things won't work out and one of you will have to get a restraining order. Thankfully, most people don't become pals under the assumption that the friendship could end one day. That's why losing a friend can be so painful. Whether it's a falling out or a slow, painful fade away, friend breakups suck, and the worst thing of all is that she's probably not ditching you because she thinks that your gluteus maximus got too maximum.

MYTH: There are no secrets between friends.

THE TRUTH: During this time of "leaked" celebrity sex tapes and YouTubing, the idea of privacy and T.M.I. is quickly going M.I.A. Just because we're quickly becoming a nation of gawkers who like to watch the everyday struggles of former child stars doesn't mean that you need to spill all the beans to your friends. Some things are better left unsaid, including, but not limited to, the fact that you have painful gas right now.

MYTH: Girls just can't get along with one another.

THE TRUTH: Let's keep the television references going, since we seem to be on a roll with them. Contrary to what fine reality programs teach us, most girls don't consider Bret Michaels someone worth ripping another girl's weave out for. We *can* all get along and cherish our female friendships. We just like to analyze our relationships. Because we're women. And it's fun. And it makes us feel like we're at least using our psychology degrees for something.

MYTH: Friends have sleepover parties that involve naked pillow fights.

THE TRUTH: Only on Cinemax at 2 AM.

Part One
Friendly Conversation

Researchers have found that unlike men, women conduct their friendships by sharing information about themselves, their feelings, and their relationships. In other words, we're all about face-to-face interaction, while our male counterparts do it side-by-side, through activities and other guy stuff. With that in mind, let's kick this estrogen-fest off with some intimate girl talk. No, we don't mean sixth-grade health class stuff. This is more like rolling up our sleeves and bringing girl code up to modern standards.

chapter one

THE FRIEND COMMANDMENTS

Ever get the silent treatment from a friend for seemingly no reason? Are you always the last to know a secret? Do you frequently apologize for your actions? If so, perhaps you need a refresher on the rules and regulations of friendship. Sure, some are so obvious that you can probably recite them in your sleep: friends don't let friends drink and dial (or, better yet, don't sleep with your BFF's boyfriend while she's in Paris for the summer with Donna and your mom just had a baby with Mel Silver). On the other hand, some rules aren't so cut and dry. In no particular order, here are the friend commandments, the rules to live by. Commit them to memory, carve them in stone, or, at the very least, hang them on your fridge next to your cable bill.

1. Thou shalt not covet thy friend's life. We all think the grass is always greener, the thighs are thinner, the diamonds are bigger, and the French fries are crispier on the other side, but don't ever allow jealousy to get the best of you.
2. That being said, thou shalt not covet thy friend's boyfriend—even if you think he's way too hot for her or, deep down, you're convinced that he is your soul mate and the two of you are really meant to be together.

Guess what: life ain't *Romeo and Juliet* or a Meg Ryan movie (you know, one of those you watch on TBS while you're hungover on a Sunday), so snap out of it, home wrecker, and go on Match.com or something.

3. Thou shalt give more than thou taketh away from a friendship.
4. Thou shalt never call thy friend up and say, "Jeff's going to be out of town this weekend, wanna hang out?"
5. Thou shalt not spread malicious gossip about a friend unless thou wants to be run over by the karma bus.
6. Thou shalt say, "Those jeans make your butt look really good." That's your story and you're sticking to it.
7. Friends don't make their friends wear seafoam green taffeta. Actually, on second thought, let's cut the shit about weddings and just be happy for one another for one day. Thou probably will get a divorce anyway.
8. Thou shalt compromise. And compromise. And compromise.
9. Thou shalt not lose touch.
10. Thou shalt not let your friend leave the house wearing Crocs, unless said friend is working in a hospital or a garden.

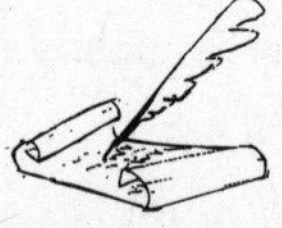

Ms. Friendship Manners

Civilization—it's what separates human beings from the other animals on this planet (with the exception of dolphins). A big part of being civilized involves the imposition of rules, regulations, laws, and treaties, but what we really want to know is if it's impolite to date a friend's ex-boyfriend. Really? Not even if he was way too good for her anyway? While we'll talk about etiquette throughout this book, here are answers to some frequent friend dilemmas. Remember: when common sense fails you, *Friend or Frenemy?*'s resident guru of politeness, Ms. Friendship Manners, will come to the rescue!

Dear Ms. Friendship Manners,

I have a bit of a dilemma. After wasting my time with a string of heinous dudes, I finally found one who delights me. (I guess if you throw enough shitheads against a wall, one will eventually stick around long enough to make you breakfast in the morning.) Anyway, there's one teeny tiny problem: my new man used to date a friend of mine. I'm torn. On one hand, I don't want to damage a friendship. On the other, you can't choose the person you love. In your opinion, is it ever kosher to get together with a friend's ex?

Waiting on the edge of my loveseat for your response,

Lovestruck in Lansing

Dear Lovestruck,

Before we get to the nitty gritty, Ms. Friendship Manners would appreciate it if you would refrain from using profanity. She also regrets that you were tortured by so many men of a fecal-headed variety. That being said, the answer to your question is *YES* and *NO*: *YES*, you should just go ahead and eat from your pal's relationship leftovers if you want to have *NO* friends.

In all seriousness, matters involving love can get rather complicated, so Ms. Friendship Manners has a complicated answer for you. Before you shift into drive and speed down Lover's Lane, you need to think with your head, rather than feel with your heart and your lady parts. Ask yourself a few questions: How serious was the relationship between your friend and this new man in your life? How much time has passed since they dated? Also, how close is your relationship with your friend? Is she the sister you never had or more like an acquaintance?

If your friend and the man had a long, passionate affair, you should quickly extricate yourself from this romantic entanglement. However, if they went on a couple of casual dates in the late nineties, Ms. Friendship Manners sees no reason why you can't have a love connection. Before making any moves, though, talk to your friend about your dilemma. Not only is it polite, but it's also the right thing to do. Keep in mind that many friends have a noncompete clause when it comes to dating. Depending on the ramifications, Mr. Wonderful might end up being more trouble than he is worth. Remember, there are plenty of male fish swimming in the sea of love, but a true friend is like a pearl, a really shiny piece of beach glass, or something else along those lines.

In closing, Miss Friendship Manners has one more point she would like to make. She respectfully disagrees with your assertion that we all suffer from Tourette's syndrome of the heart. She believes that while we might not always be able to choose how we feel about another person, we can control our actions. Case in point: Do you know who once said, "The heart wants what it wants"? It was Woody Allen, and we all know what happened after his heart got what it wanted: *Hollywood Ending* and *Melinda and Melinda.*

chapter two

THROUGH THE YEARS

A Timeline of Semi-recent Triumphs and Tragedies in Girlfriend History

Before we examine the current state of your friendships, let's take a look back at the past. Regardless of what you believe about the origin of human life (i.e., we were molded in the likeness of a higher power, evolved from monkeys, grew from the remnants of the Big Bang, or were purchased in bulk at Sam's Club), one thing is undisputable: as soon as there were two women on Earth, the first question asked was "Does this fig leaf make my ass look fat?" From that moment on, women have been making one another laugh and cry and have been overanalyzing one another's actions. Let's take a look at some other triumphs and tragedies in the history of our friendships.

1870 The first formally recognized sorority, Kappa Alpha Theta at DePauw University, sets up shop. Unfortunately, the permanent marker has yet to be invented so the sisters have to circle the pledges' fat and other various body flaws with quill pens.

1876 Alexander Graham Bell introduces the first working telephone. His wife then uses it to call her best friend and ask her what bonnet she's wearing to tea tomorrow.

1888 The Kodak camera makes its debut and women everywhere perfect the ubiquitous "best friend" shot, which is captured by putting one arm around your BFF, smiling until it hurts, and then stretching out your free arm as far as possible and snapping a scary closeup photo of the two of you that you will later trash because it's so unflattering. Seriously, not even a supermodel looks good from that angle.

1904 The answering machine allows people to figure out who's calling by listening to their incoming message (for example, "I know you're there bitch, pick up the phone"). The answering machine remains the most popular method of call screening until 1988, when BellSouth begins the first commercial application of caller ID, a great deterrent for that creepy guy you met at the bar last night and gave your phone number to in a weak moment. Unfortunately, they had to go and invent a way to block caller ID.

1910 Hallmark helps people communicate their feelings, connect with each other, and celebrate milestones. In 1919, the introduction of friendship-themed cards makes the greeting card section more foreign to men than the feminine hygiene aisle.

1912 Juliette Gordon Low organizes the first Girl Scout troop in Savannah, Georgia. Girl Scout meetings quickly become one of the few places where a girl purposely wears the same outfit as all of her friends.

1928 Fred Rogers, star of the PBS show *Mister Rogers' Neighborhood* is born. While lacking any sort of plot, the show featured various interactions between friends both in the real world and the world of make-believe. It taught children peaceful ways of dealing with hurt and angry feelings, in addition to the importance of a good cardigan sweater and a comfy pair of sneakers. This kind, neighborly soul passed away in 2003.

1935 Congress declares the first Sunday in August to be National Friendship Day.

1940 With the men off fighting in World War II, more than six million American women enter the workforce. Unfortunately, *Grey's Anatomy*, *American Idol*, HBO, and Britney Spears don't exist, so the water cooler conversation is kind of boring.

1948 The first ever Tupperware party was held, pioneering the concept of getting women together to buy crap that they don't need. Decades later women continue to employ the original direct marketing strategy, only the Tupperware has been replaced with "romance enhancements" and "relationship aids." Translation: dildos and butt beads.

1959 Mattel launches Barbie, the doll that promotes 0 percent body fat and the importance of having several cars including a convertible, a Jeep, and a van. In 1963, Barbie began to accumulate a posse of diverse friends starting with Midge (she was brunette and, frankly, a little XXY); Francie, Barbie's first African American BFF; and Share a Smile Becky, who rolled in a hot pink wheelchair.

1966 Jacqueline Susann pens *Valley of the Dolls*, launching a million book clubs.

1970 The first Lucille Roberts opens. Leotard- and leg-warmer-clad women could now bond over outdated workout equipment.

1976 Laverne and Shirley become television's first female example of nonsexual life partners. "Schlemiel! Schlemazel! Hasenpfeffer Incorporated!"

1985 *The Golden Girls*, the first senior all-female television family, gives women (and some gay men) a reason to look forward to their older years when all the guys are dead and they can hang out in loose-fitting, bright-colored knitwear and eat cheesecake late into the night.

1986 "That's What Friends Are For" wins a Grammy for Song of the Year and Best Pop Performance for a Duo or a Group, and becomes a requisite for bat mitzvahs, school dances, and sweet sixteen parties.

1988 Female friendships strike it big at the box office with the release of *Beaches* (tagline: "Friends come and go but there's always one you're stuck with for life") and *Working Girl*. *Beaches* captivates audiences with the schmaltzy story of unlikely best friends (and Barbara Hershey's collagen-enhanced trout pout), while *Working Girl* examines women in the workplace and sets a new standard for commuter chic.

1992 A British engineer sends the first commercial text message. He wasn't drunk, nor did he write, "c u 2nite. K?"

1994 *Friends* debuts on NBC and reaffirms the belief that at least some men and women (okay, Phoebe and Joey) can just be friends and with the right hairstyle you can marry Brad Pitt.

1996 Girl Power! The Spice Girls' first single, "Wannabe," becomes the best-selling single by a female group in history, selling more than six million copies worldwide. The hook—"If you wannabe my lover / you've gotta get with my friends / Make it last forever / friendship never ends"—still doesn't make any sense. (Are they talking about a threesome? Shouldn't he just meet my friends for tapas or something?)

1997 Linda Tripp begins taping conversations in which Monica Lewinsky details her alleged affair with President Clinton. Tripp then uses the tapes to blow up Lewinsky's spot (sorry, poor choice of words).

1998 *Sex and the City* premieres on HBO. The show encourages women to have frank discussions about sex, consume copious amounts of alcohol, speak in clever puns, and wear tutus as skirts, underwear as shorts, and men's shirts as dresses.

1999 The BlackBerry allows people to stay connected to their e-mail 24/7, which earns it the nickname CrackBerry.

2004 A dark year in friendship history. Both *Sex and the City* and *Friends* air their final episodes.

July 2005 Rupert Murdoch's News Corporation announces that it will acquire Intermix Media, parent company of social networking giant MySpace, for $580 million. Tila Tequila's boobs rejoiced.

Spring 2006 Real-life "Mean Girls" take over Hollywood when a video of Paris Hilton giggling as her friend Brandon Davis goes on a tirade about Lindsay Lohan's "firecrotch" hits the Internet and Denise Richards starts dating Richie Sambora, the soon-to-be ex-husband of her supposed best friend, Heather Locklear.

Summer 2006 Oprah and Gayle's Big "Not Gay" Adventure starts in Santa Barbara, California, and ends ten days and 3,600 miles later in New York City, just in time for the Tony Awards (we can't think of anything less gay than the Tony Awards).

Fall 2006 Paris Hilton (yes, we just had to add her to this timeline twice) has a bone to pick with her former BFF Nicole Richie. The world lets out a collective sigh of relief when the two make up over a steak dinner about a year later. In 2008 the duo becomes the ultimate best friend cliché when they date twin brothers Benji and Joel Madden

Spring 2007 There are eight million CrackBerry subscribers. While it's an impressive number of people, they are still no match for one angry Naomi Campbell.

July 2007 Researchers find that obesity can spread among close friends. We're sure that there's a joke in here somewhere, but we'll let it be because this is just too damn freaky.

December 2007 Match.com launches Match My Friends, which allows people to create profiles for their friends and search for potential dates on their behalf, putting Jewish mothers out of business.

March 2008 The season three premiere of MTV's *The Hills* draws its biggest audience ever, with 4.8 million viewers tuning in to watch Lauren "LC" Conrad and Heidi "Trout Power" Montag recite their lines.

chapter three

TEXTUAL HEALING

The New Rules of Digital Engagement

Sometime after the advent of the Internet and before Steve Jobs packaged our lives into sleek little titanium and white plastic boxes, we became e-ddicted: hooked on instant communication and online interaction. It all happened so fast. One minute we had dicey dial-up connections and car phones that we kept in our glove compartments just in case of roadside emergencies, and the next we were surfing the Web with warp-speed wireless networks and keeping our teensy cells within reach just in case one of life's little emergencies popped up, like walking down the street or waiting in line at Starbucks.

As we brought up earlier, text messaging, e-mail, and a host of gadgets that ring and ding can do wonderful things for our friendships, such as enhancing current relationships, forming new bonds, and reestablishing old ones. We also mentioned the flip side of the flip-phone phenomenon: digital communication is a good supplement to good old-fashioned face-to-face interaction, but it's no substitution, which all seems simple enough, but some people obviously don't understand.

With the digital communication explosion also comes a new set of rules, regulations, social norms, and expectations. Read on to find out how to make the most of it all and not become one of *those* people. (You know who we're talking about—the phone zombies who sit together at brunch but aren't *all there* as they text away on their cells with that same glassy-eyed stare that your little brother gets as he sits in front of PlayStation.)

Virtual Insanity: Friendship Mutations in the Digital Age

In addition to a whole new set of rules and regulations, the digital explosion has also affected your friends and brought out entirely new facets of their personalities. Here's how to deal with the technophiles, technophobes, and everyone in between.

✦ **The Cellebutard**: The Cellebutard needs to stop getting her news from *Star* magazine and *In Touch*. (*People* "has too many words.") At some point, a steady diet of pop culture junk food has convinced her that blowing through her anytime minutes while she's on the elliptical, at the movies, waiting in line at the supermarket—hell, probably even in the stirrups at the gyn—makes her seem as important as the quasi-starlets who grace the "celebs are just like us!" pages of the tabloids with UGGs on their feet, a giant skim soy milk latte in one hand, and a phone in the other.

No matter how personal the conversation, the Cellebutard prefers yapping on her phone as loudly and as publicly as possible. In fact, she doesn't care (or is painfully unaware) that everyone within a half-mile radius knows that lately, she's been experiencing a burning sensation when she pees. The Cellebutard hasn't always been such a phone whore. It just seems like she got caught up in everything and now, all you can hope for is that Promises in Malibu develops a twelve-step program for digital addiction.

How to deal: Since it isn't very likely that you will find a restaurant about a hundred feet underground where cell service is as sketchy as that guy who graduated two years before you but still hung out at all the high school parties, next time you're out with the Cellebutard, try to wean her off her phone in one of two ways. Either kindly ask her to power down in your presence, because it's rude and inconsiderate to talk on the phone while you are trying to enjoy your sushi, or, if that doesn't work, resort to some tough love and grab her BlackBerry and threaten to go all Naomi Campbell on her ass. (Yes, she's worth another mention.)

✦ **The Technophile:** The Technophile lives for the latest and greatest electronic gadgets or e-innovations. Nothing, not even a natural disaster or a case of *E. coli,* will keep her from sleeping outside the Apple store to get her hands on the latest iCrap. While you may have been the first in your crew to rock leggings or ankle booties, the Technophile has been paying her bills online, getting her movies through Netflix, and posting clips on YouTube since before you even knew what a Shuffle was.

How to deal: On the bright side, the Technophile is always plugged in, so she's very easy to stay in contact with. She's also a good friend to have because if you ever have any technological issues, she's like your own personal Geek Squad. However, be prepared, because she expects everyone else to be as technically inclined and reachable as she is.

✦ **The Techno-Indignant:** You know that we are living in a digital world but she is far from a digital girl—or that's what she wants everyone to think. The Techno-Indignant enjoys playing the contrarian. Not only does she whine about the evils of technology, but she's also *that person* who waxes poetic about listening to her tunes on wax (*vinyl is the only way to really experience recorded music*), thinks she deserves a medal because she doesn't watch TV, and refuses to dress up for Halloween. Yes, she (reluctantly) owns a cell phone (she was the last in your group of friends to get one) and has access to e-mail (she checks it weekly). However, you can never reach her when you need to. It's probably because the Techno-Indignant is too busy pretending to listen to NPR and read *The New Yorker*.

How to deal: We hear that Best Buy is having a special on carrier pigeons. If that doesn't work, go throw a rock against the Techno-Indignant's bedroom window if you need to get her attention.

✦ **The E-Incompetent:** While the Techno-Indignant likes to pretend that she doesn't "get" the whole digital communication thing, the E-Incompetent really is completely clueless about technology. It's one thing when your parents still use AOL and a have painfully slow dial-up connection. However, it's quite another situation when someone your own age doesn't know the difference between "forward" and "reply." After you moved to a new apartment, you sent out an e-mail to your entire address book with your updated contact information. Not surprisingly, the E-Incompetent replied to all with an attachment that contained the Teddy Bear virus.

How to deal: It's best to stick to what the E-Incompetent knows best and give her a call if you ever need to talk to her. Just try to ignore the fact that she's the only person who still thinks it's cool to have "Für Elise" or "The Entertainer" as her ring tone.

- **The Private Eye–Book:** The Private Eye–Book is a Googler extraordinaire, a cybersleuth worthy of her own *CSI* spin-off show. With a few keystrokes, she can pull up the registry of your middle school crush and his fiancée (who the hell needs a $150 panini press from Williams-Sonoma?) or find out what happened to that girl who allegedly got a little friendly with the whole varsity football team in the back of the bus after an away game (she and her minister husband run a church youth group in Utah) all before you even have your second cup of coffee for the day. If you need to get the dirt on an ex-boyfriend, ex-roommate, or that cute new temp in the marketing department, the Private Eye–Book will deliver the goods.

  How to deal: While she's an excellent detective, make it a point to stay on the Private Eye–Book's good side, because somewhere lurking in the darkest corners of cyberspace there are photos of you before your nose job. (Deviated septum, our ass.)

- **The T.M.I.-er:** If you want to know what she had for breakfast last Tuesday, what base she reached last night with the new guy she's dating, or what her cleavage looks like from a variety of different angles, you're in luck. The T.M.I.-er documents the minute details of her life on a blog and also provides hourly updates regarding her emotional state on her MySpace page.

How to deal: The T.M.I.-er just wants attention, so it's probably best to ignore her online exhibitionism. However, if people start talking about her online escapades behind her back, you might want to mention a recent article you read about a woman who got fired from her job after her employer found less than ladylike posts on her MySpace page. (Hey, it's not exactly a lie. We're sure it must have happened before.) Or you could simply tell her that unless she's thinking about becoming a Hooters waitress, she should probably remove photos of her chi-chis from her site.

- **The Blast from the Past:** Whether she lived next door when you were a kid or she snored away in the bunk above you at summer camp, you haven't heard from the Blast from the Past since you got your first period. Then, one day, thanks to the wonders of technology, she e-mails or Facebook messages you out of nowhere. At first, you're surprised to hear from her. Then, after covering the basics (where you live, what you do, and what's going on with the other girls who used hang in your crew in middle school) there's pretty much nothing left to talk about.

  How to deal: While it's great to get back in touch with old friends, if your newly reconnected relationship exists only in cyberspace and you don't have any new experiences together, chances are that the past will stay in the past. (Or will the past be the future? Or will the future be the past? Our heads hurt. Let's just say that there are only so many times that you and the Blast from the Past can talk about that one time at band camp when Lauren Anderson shat in the lake.)

Contact Highs and Lows: The Good, the Bad, and the Ugly of Digital Communication

Way before Y2K, Napster, and the proliferation of junk e-mails with subject lines such as "XXX maKE iT rOcK HarD XXX" and "lose 10lbs in 10 seconds," you actually had to be in a certain place at a certain time if you wanted to communicate with your friends. Now you can be just about anywhere and stay connected to the world around you. It sounds nice in theory, but in reality the digital revolution pressures us to be accessible to everyone, wherever and whenever. Our ability to be in constant touch has made us more dependent on technology than Barbara Walters is on soft lighting. Luckily, your cell, text, and e-mail account are more helpful than they are harmful when it comes to your friendships—that is, as long as you follow some simple guidelines. Read on for the good, the bad, and the ugly of digital communication, along with the oh-so-important rules of engagement.

Cell Phones

Weighing in at just over three ounces, today's cells are a mere shadow of their former barbell-heavy ancestors. (Remember Zack's portable brick-sized phone on *Saved by the Bell*?) Thanks to your mobile, you can easily let Mom know that your flight landed safely in Florida or send a picture of your new niece to a bunch of people in your address book who couldn't care less. Cell phones aren't just a tool of convenience; they're a way of life. (Deep stuff, right?)

The Good: We're always reachable.
The Bad and the Ugly: We're always reachable.

The Rules of Engagement:

• Refrain from engaging in a lengthy, personal conversation with a friend on your cell phone when you should be engaging in a lengthy, personal conversation with a friend who is sitting across from you at dinner (and is pretending that she isn't annoyed).

• Use your cell phone to do good, like reporting a hit-and-run accident, snapping an incriminating pic of the pervert who flashed you his twig and berries on the bus, or letting your BFF know that there's a new flavor of low-fat ice cream at Häagen-Dazs.

• Give friends and other loved ones at least twenty-four hours to respond to a voice-mail message before you go all ape shit on them.

• Turn your cell off every few days as a self-imposed detox. Once you get past the cold sweats, chills, and nausea, you might be surprised at what a little bit of space can do for a friendship.

• If you must talk on your cell phone in a public place, use your six-inch voice. However, if you're talking about sex stuff, feel free to entertain everyone around you.

• Do yourself a favor and actually memorize some of the important numbers in your cell—or at least write them down on paper. This way, the next time you drop your phone in a toilet, you won't have to send out an e-mail to all of the people in your address book, pleading for their contact info.

Text Messaging

C U in 5. K? What was once poor grammar is now a highly evolved language reserved for text messaging. It's no surprise that texting has it's own lingo, considering that it's the most widely used mobile data service on the planet, with 72 percent of all mobile phone users joining in on the fun (or so it says on Wikipedia).

The Good: Instead of shouting into your cell in a crowded restaurant or jamming your finger in your ear so you can hear the person on the other end of the line, text messaging allows you to send and receive information regardless of how noisy (or quiet) your location. Plus, it serves as a relatively nonintrusive way to communicate important details to your friends, like that you just saw a girl wearing stirrup pants and a banana clip in her hair.

The Bad and the Ugly: A recent study at the University of Queensland, Australia, has found that text messaging is just as addictive as crack. Actually, they didn't find that at all. They found that texting is just as addictive as cigarette smoking, but we'll bet all of Whitney's Grammys that it's a lot like crack, too.

The Rules of Engagement:

- Keep your texts short and breezy. Text messages are not the appropriate form of communication for major declarations such as "I'm really a *he*" or "I'm in love with your boyfriend." Save those types of conversations for a more formal environment such as your Facebook Wall or instant messenger.
- Text your friends during their normal hours of operation. Just because you still booze it up on a school night like a rock star worth of his or her own *Behind the Music* episode doesn't mean your more responsible friends want to be woken up by the *beep-beep* of their message indicator at 2 AM only to read "what r u doin? i m so wasted. woooooo!!!!!!"
- Remember: Friends don't let friends text and drive, drink and text, or drink and drive.

?!? *Pop Quiz:* R U a Txt Addct? ?!?

Do you need an intervention for your text habit? Take this quiz and find out if you're hooked or merely a recreational user.

1. **Fill in the blank. T9 is ___.**
   a. The greatest timesaver since *8 Minute Abs.*
   b. A neat idea in theory, but I can never get the darn thing to work.
   c. Not nearly as good as *T3: Rise of the Machines.*
2. **Texting while sexing: yea or nay?**
   a. Yea, yea, yea!
   b. That's just nay-sty.
3. **Is there something vibrating in your jeans or are you just happy to see us?**
   a. Just a sec—my shit is blowing up.
   b. So that's where I left my Pocket Rocket!
   c. You must be feeling my chakra and life force energy.
4. **True or false: Swarovski-crystal bejeweled BlackBerries.**
   a. True
   b. False
5. **You just realized that you misplaced your cell phone/ BlackBerry/Treo/iPhone and will have to survive an entire evening without it. Which Kelly Clarkson song best sums up your feelings about the situation?**
   a. "Miss Independent"
   b. "Since U Been Gone"
   c. "Never Again"
6. **Admit it. You've been enticed by those television commercials that hawk musical ring tones.**

a. As if! That scam is along the lines of Miss Cleo or the Psychic Friends Network.

b. I've been morbidly fascinated, but never took it a step further.

c. Only once, but I was drunk. I swear.

7. **You just sent a text to a friend and haven't heard back yet. (It's been fifteen minutes.) Rate your indignation in the rock 'n' roll scale.**

a Grateful Dead mellow

b. Cradle of Filth kill-everyone-and-bury-'em-in-your-backyard-style anger

c. Hot Topic mall angst

8. **If the world as we know it was just about to end a la the 2004 classic film *The Day After Tomorrow* and you had time to send only one text message, who would you send it to and what would it say?**

a. My mom. I'd tell her I love her.

b. A group message to as many family members, friends, acquaintances, coworkers, and ex-boyfriends as my cell phone would allow. I'd tell them to be strong and I'll see them on the other side.

c. Screw text messaging! I'd find Jake Gyllenhaal and make some sweet apocalyptic love.

9. **Have you ever gotten a case of "numb thumb"?**

a. Once, when I was ten years old and went on a weeklong Super Mario Bros. bender.

b. Nope. I have full feeling in all of my digits.

c. Yes, but I consider it a victory because I've texted through the pain.

10. **Complete the following analogy: I : Texting ::**

a. Lifetime : Movies starring Melissa Gilbert or Meredith Baxter

b. MTV : Music

c. Bravo : Straight male viewers

Answer Key:

1. a: 3; b: 2; c: 3
2. a: 3; b: 1
3. a: 3; b: 2; c: 1
4. a: 1; b: 3
5. a: 1; b: 2; c: 3
6. a: 1; b: 2; c: 3
7. a: 1; b: 3; c: 2
8. a: 1; b: 2; c: 3
9. a: 2; b: 1; c: 3
10. a: 3; b: 2; c:1

If You Scored:

10 to 14: Straight Edge

You'd rather have a conversation than *type* a conversation. Fair enough. Just keep in mind that texting can be pretty darn convenient and it's a lot less annoying than yelling "CAN YOU HEAR ME NOW?" into the phone when you're trying to have a chat in a crowded location. Try it sometime—everybody's doin' it.

15 to 23: A Recreational User

You have a normal, healthy, and functioning text life. Just make sure to engage in safe texting.

23 to 30: A Raging Text Addict

If you were bleeding to death, you'd probably try to text 911. While there's nothing wrong with having enthusiasm for technology, you take it to another level, salivating like Pavlov's dog every time your cell phone dings with a new message. Once in a while, give your thumbs a rest and try actually *talking* to rather than *typing* back and forth with a real live person?.

E-mail

In our opinion, e-mail is one of the most significant modern inventions, right up there with the Epilady and hundred-calorie snack packs. (It really is all about portion control, ladies.) E-mail enables you to correspond with friends and family who live far away but aren't worth the long-distance bill. It also makes work a lot easier—or, we should say, it makes it a lot easier to pretend you're doing work at your place of work, when you're actually e-mailing back and forth with your boyfriend.

The Good: E-mail is an immediate form of communication that doesn't always have to be immediate. Okay, that probably seems like it makes no sense, but let us explain. If you sometimes wish that you had the ability to freeze time by touching the tips of your fingers like Evie from *Out of this World,* you can—sort of—with e-mail. Unlike a face-to-face conversation or a chat over the phone, e-mail doesn't require that you respond right away, giving you the chance to consult your life coach/Ouija board/cat before composing a message. Then, once you hit SEND, your message reaches your respondent's mailbox immediately, unlike a good, old-fashioned letter.

The Bad and the Ugly: Since you don't get the chance to hear the sender's tone of voice, see her facial gestures, or observe her body language—all cues that help the person on the receiving end of a message better understand its context and meaning—e-mail is one form of communication that is very open to *mis*interpretation. Unless you are very familiar with a friend's writing style, humor and other nuances don't usually come across very well in e-mail. Let's not even get into those people WHO WRITE EVERYTHING IN ALL CAPS.

Another reason why e-messages sometimes get lost in translation is because of dreaded "multitasking." We're usually in a hurry when we are writing, reading, and responding to messages, making it easier to misread, miscomprehend, and make really embarrassing typos. People who are sending us e-mail are doing the same exact thing. This is why you fly into a frenzy and think that you did something wrong when a normally verbose friend suddenly gives curt, one-word responses to your e-mails. In reality, she's busy doing a bunch of things at once: cooking pasta on the stove, writing up some reports for work, and watching one of those freaky specials on TLC about some Siamese twin babies who also have gigantism, flesh-eating tumors, and genius IQs.

The Rules of Engagement:

- Avoid putting anything in an e-mail that you wouldn't say to someone's face, since whatever you write in a message can be forwarded around cyberspace and eventually end up on Gawker. Also, you know how you should never go to bed angry? Well, don't e-mail angry, either. While it's tempting to respond fast and furiously type out words like *hobag, bizzo,* and *dirty, dirty slut,* once you click SEND, your e-mail is gone, along with your friendship. And, even if the two of you kiss and make up, she'll have a constant reminder in her in-box of your anger, pettiness, and potty mouth.

• Always put *something* in the subject line, even if it's just a simple, "I'm sleeping with your man." Otherwise, no subject = no reason to read your e-mail.

• Limit your use of the high priority option. Save the freak-outs for real emergencies and don't write "PLEASE HELP ME, SOMEBODY" "Big Emergency!" or "Redrum" in a subject line if you simply can't decide whether to have tuna or chicken salad for lunch.

• E-mail can be very casual, but you should default to a salutation that is a bit more formal than "hey beyotch" if you don't know someone very well.

What Your Friends' Obsessive E-mail Forwarding Habits Say About Them

There's actually one other type of friend that has emerged from the digital age: the Obsessive Forwarder. The Obsessive Forwarder likes to clog up your in-box with every type of forward that comes her way. This is what the OF's favorite types of e-mail forwards say about her personality:

- Anything featuring cute photos of puppies, kitties, and/or babies = I'm not getting any.
- Lame gender-based jokes about men never listening, neglecting to do the dishes, or forgetting to put down the toilet seat = Remember how I used to be all wild and, dare I say, a bit slutty, but it didn't matter because I was the life

of the party? Well, now that I've found a boyfriend who doesn't live in his mother's basement and spend all day eating 'shrooms and watching Adult Swim, you need to understand that *that girl never existed*. You got it? And when he's around, don't even *think* about bringing up that one time on Spring Break in Acapulco.

- Alarmist articles about traces of the Ebola virus discovered in jars of peanut butter and shrapnel found in pizza rolls or takes on the classic cautionary tale about the daughter of a friend of a friend's mother's coworker who was almost kidnapped in a mall parking lot because she wore her hair in a long ponytail = I'm off my anxiety meds.
- "I'm so glad we're friends" forwards = I'm too busy to actually talk to you.
- Chain letters promising love, good luck, or free iPod nanos if you forward the e-mails to at least ten other people in your address book = Get your financials in order because I'm about to hit you up for a loan.
- Wacky YouTube videos = I'm high.
- Photoshop gems that are totally NSFW (*not safe for work,* for you technophobes) yet lack prior warning that opening them up in an office environment is probably a bad idea = I'm jealous of your success and want to get you fired.
- Poems and stories containing unsolicited and unexpected religious undertones = You think I'm a good listener but I'm actually silently judging you.
- Embarrassing e-mails that were written by people you know and were obviously not meant for the entire cyber-world to read = Don't feel left out. I forward along your e-mails behind your back, too.

- Messages containing huge WAV and video files that tie up your e-mail for what feels like hours on end = I have no idea how to use a computer.
- Political rants = I don't actually vote.

Social Networking and Virtual Communities

MySpace, Facebook, and the host of other social networking sites out there are the grown-up version of hanging out at the mall with your BFFs—all 325 of them. They allow you to connect and reconnect with friends, collect buddies like Garbage Pail Kids, and judge people about their tastes in music, movies, and hobbies. Whether you have a profile to showcase your craft (that is, your boobies) or you signed on to stalk your ex-boyfriend, there's no denying that social networking is a bigger time-suck than the Proactiv infomercials.

The Good: Your social networking site of choice is like your own personalized CNN. You can find out who got dumped, who got a new job, and who's moving to Paris to "find herself," just by clicking on their profiles. Also, you can "poke" someone without getting sued for sexual harassment or you can get poked without running the risk of getting pregnant or an STD. Pretty neat.

The Bad and the Ugly: News travels fast online, especially if the news is that your boss gave you a pink slip, your boyfriend gave you the boot, or your hairdresser gave you a bowl haircut instead of the Posh Spice bob that you requested. Another potential downer: if you're spending all of your time talking about what you're doing online rather than what you're doing in real life, you might not have a real life anymore.

The Rules of Engagement:

• Be selective about which friend requests you approve. Okay, you don't have to be a total snob about it, but do you really need to be online buds with fourteen-year-old emo boy from Iowa who found you because, big surprise, he also lists *The Nightmare Before Christmas* and *Amélie* as his favorite movies?

• Do set a time limit for your cyber-stalking sessions.

• Remember that you aren't that fourteen-year-old emo boy from Iowa, so you should online network accordingly. And, if you are fourteen years old, you shouldn't be reading this book. Try *Harry Potter* instead or go do your homework, young man!

• Don't rely on MySpace/Facebook/whateversocialnetworkingsite.com to make last-minute plans and then get mad when no one shows up at your fund-raiser for irritable bowel syndrome.

• Take your arguments outside of cyberspace. Fighting in the comments section of your profile makes you look petty and childish. Instead, do what grownups do and settle any misunderstanding face-to-face: slap the bitch next time you see her out at a bar.

Evites

Electronic invitations are a convenient way to gather a bunch of people together in one place for an evening so they all have to pretend that they like one another.

The Good: Evites are cheap, fast, and environmentally friendly. (Al Gore would approve!)

The Bad and the Ugly: Most of us have experienced unnecessary anxiety and the occasional existential crisis when dealing with Evites, which makes us wonder if it was easier back when

Mom just bought a twenty-four-pack of Rainbow Brite invitations and sent them to everyone in our class. There's some worry about which design to choose—generic party girls sipping cosmopolitans or the picture of the pink birthday cake? Then, there's the fact that you obsessively check the invite for responses. (*It's been two minutes, why is no one replying yet? Why don't I have any friends? Am I going to die alone?!*) Add onto the stress pile the pressure to come up with a guest list long enough that it has to be compressed. And there's also pressure to perform when you receive an Evite. You can't just write "yes" or "no" as a response to an invitation. You have to be witty or snarky or include an inside joke that only the party's organizer will understand and will show everyone else on the invite list that you aren't just another seat filler. (*I might not be able to make it because the old man moved my cheese and then I need to knit a sweater and go dancing. Yeah, cats!*)

The Rules of Engagement

- Send Evites for major celebrations such as birthdays, anniversaries, and sex change fund-raisers. For more formal occasions, you should send paper invitations in the mail.
- Don't forward an Evite to the known world without first asking the organizer if it's okay.
- Write down essential information about the party beforehand (location, address, start time) so you don't become one of the dozens of people who will call the organizer five minutes before the event and ask her to relay said details.

Photo-Sharing Web Sites

It's Martha Stewart's dream: a way to view and organize photos that doesn't involve dusty shoeboxes, bent corners, or glue-gunning your fingers together. (Actually, that's us. We're sure Martha is a regular whiz with a glue gun.) Photo-sharing Web sites such as Kodak Gallery, Snapfish, and Flickr let you show off your vacation, wedding, or new puppy to all of your friends.

The Bad and the Ugly: Unless you actually take and upload the photos yourself, these sites are a bit like your own personal paparazzi. There's the potential that total strangers can see a rather unflattering pic of you in a bathing suit after you just ate a five-course meal while on vacation in Mexico. (Of course, you waited forty-five minutes before you went swimming.)

The Rules of Engagement:

- Do yourself and your friends a favor, and edit out any dirty or hideous photos before you upload them. Save the worst photos for blackmail material.
- Don't get all crazy if people don't immediately look at the photo album you created that contains 118 images of your newborn third cousin in a pumpkin costume.
- Just like Evites, you might want to ask the creator of the photo album before you forward the link to the known universe.

Ten Ways to Detox from Your Digital Habit

Whether you're a hardcore digital addict who gets the shakes when your Wi-Fi is down, a compulsive CrackBerryer with carpal tunnel, or an obsessive social networker, everyone needs to log off of their virtual reality and see their friends in person once in awhile. There's a quaint charm in a local bar, coffee shop, café, and so on, where everyone knows your real name as opposed to the one you use online. Actually, it's so retro and quirky that it seems like a

Wes Anderson movie, which is actually kind of cool. Here are some good old-fashioned ways to have fun—no password required.

1. Take a walk without brining along a handheld electronic device. (Yes, that includes those *Star Trek*–ish Bluetooth thingies you attach to your ear).
2. Go on a camping trip with your inner circle. The first person who bitches about the lack of a cell signal in the woods has to drink unboiled stream water and eat wild mushrooms.
3. Organize a board game night. Hide your laptop so no one can Google a questionable Scrabble word or find out what Monopoly aficionados have to say about the legitimacy of building five houses and three hotels on Boardwalk.
4. Get a manicure without using your cell or BlackBerry. Bonus points if you can hold out until your nails are completely dry. (FYI: that is thirty full minutes).
5. Take one of those Polaroid instant cameras out with you and your friends. Marvel at the joy of a photograph that you can actually hold in your hand.
6. Send your parents their anniversary card via snail mail. Despite what they say, they have no idea how to open an e-card and haven't been able to read a card from you since 1999. P.S. Don't forget to add a stamp. P.P.S. Postage right now for a standard letter is like $12.50 or something.
7. Go for cocktails with your BFF and bitch about your other friends behind their backs, as opposed to doing it via e-mail or text message.

8. Plan a reunion for the friends in your "Camp Shady Hills" Facebook network. It's more proactive than staring longingly at their profiles.
9. Invite your most stylish friend on a day trip to the nearest shopping outlet. Sure, you'll have to deal with crowds and unhelpful sales people (an undeniable bonus of online shopping) but her fashion advice will be totally worth it.
10. Spend your lunch hour actually eating lunch, preferably with your coworkers. Not only is breaking bread a good way to bond with your fellow employees, but you'll also get better office gossip from them over $7 paninis than over IM.

Your CliffsNotes for Social Interaction

Digital communication has definitely blurred the lines between casual and formal, appropriate and inappropriate, and the familiar and the unfamiliar. For instance, is e-mail the appropriate way to decline a friend's request to join her and her boyfriend in a threesome? Below, we've a created a bit of a cheat sheet. Think of it like CliffsNotes (those things that saved your ass when your sophomore English class was reading *Beowulf*), only for social interactions. Here's how it works: We give a situation and then indicate the bare minimum form of communication you should employ. But don't forget that a phone call or a handwritten card are always best, especially when the person is a close friend or family member.

 This definitely warrants a phone call

 Send some good old-fashioned snail mail.

 E-mail is totally acceptable.

 Tell 'em face-to-face.

 A text message should suffice.

Extending Invitations

You're trying to get your friends together for dinner/a movie/ happy hour on Friday.

You want to ask out that cute guy from the gym.

You're planning a function that requires women to wear Spanx and men to don ties.

You want to meet up with a former coworker to catch up and do some networking.

It's 2 AM on a Saturday morning and you're looking for someone with whom to engage in frisky behavior that you will probably regret as soon as the sun comes up.

Expressing Sympathy, Giving Condolences, or Wishing Others Well

A member of your friend's immediate family has passed away.

A celeb has died.

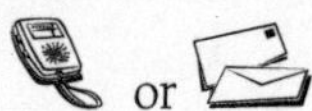

A celeb has died, and as a result, you have won an office death pool and you want to gloat and make those suckas pay up.

Your friend's family member/close relative is seriously ill.

Your friend is hungover or is experiencing intestinal distress after eating some rank seafood or those mystery

Chinese leftovers that were in the back of her fridge. You told her not to eat them and she did, so you don't want to say "I told you so" but you want to seem caring, too.

Showing Thanks

Someone got you a wedding present.

Your nana sent you a birthday check.

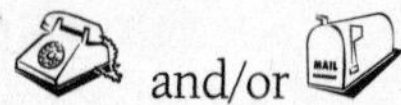

A friend got you a birthday present.

A friend got you a really, really, really expensive birthday present.

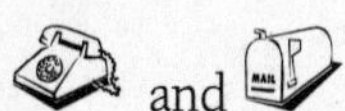

A friend stayed up with you all night and patiently listened while you drunkenly sobbed and rambled about your ex-boyfriend.

Happy Holidays and Other Celebrations and Congratulations

You want to wish a friend happy holidays or happy birthday.

 or

You want to wish a friend a happy made-up holiday like Sweetest Day.

A friend gets engaged.

 or 

A friend gets engaged for the fifth time.

It's Personal

Breaking up with a boyfriend

Breaking up with a friend

 or

Telling your boyfriend that the EPT was negative

Informing a hookup that his services are no longer needed

Letting your parents know that you're moving in with your boyfriend

Letting your parents know that you're moving in with your girlfriend

Ms. Friendship Manners

Dear Ms. Friendship Manners,

How soon after your friend has a baby are you obligated to see it?

Sincerely,
Babyphobic in Bayside

Dear Babyphobic,

People generally fall into three categories: babyphobic, babyaholic, and the rest of us. Judging by your pen name, Ms. Friendship Manners concludes that you must be pediatrically challenged. Here's the thing: if your friend just had a child, you need to show your support as soon as possible. The arrival of a little one is one of the biggest events that has happened in her life or that can happen in anyone's life, for that matter, with the exception of that family from all the TLC specials who lives in Arkansas, has eighteen kids, and needs to drive to the supermarket in a school bus.

A word of advice to the babyphobics, babyaholics, and everyone else: Do not be offended if your friend isn't feeling up to hitting the discotheque right after she gave birth. Children change the dynamic of every friendship, but so what? Stop thinking about yourself and ask her how she is doing and pay her a visit when she feels up to it. It would also be polite if you offered to baby-sit for an afternoon so your friend could get out of the house and treat herself to a new hairdo. Yes, Ms. Friendship Manners stole this from an episode of *Sex and the City*.

If the whole baby situation still makes you feel a bit squeamish and uncomfortable, don't forget about back in college when you had your wisdom teeth extracted and your friends stopped by to eat ice cream and watch bad movies with you. Not to be rude, but you looked like H-E-Double-Hockysticks warmed over, bloody gauze, and all. Your friends still stayed by your side. If you paid attention in sex ed class, you know that a baby is a lot bigger than a wisdom tooth and the birth canal is not your mouth. Yes, your friend needs you right now.

Part Two
Your Buddy List:
The People in Your Social Stratosphere

Friends come in all shapes, sizes, and colors, but in this section of the book, we identify the most common friendly (and non-friendly) archetypes and show how to relate to them in a variety of settings. Forget a village. It takes a small army to make up the many layers of your social circle.

chapter four

WE ARE FRAMILY

Your Closest Confidantes

A wise man once said (okay, we found it on Google): "True friends are like diamonds—precious and rare. False friends are like autumn leaves—found everywhere." We like to think along dirtier lines: Good friends are like orgasms. You're lucky enough to have one and *really* lucky if you have multiple ones.

While all friends are valuable in their own ways, only a select group is willing to wait for hours with you in the emergency room after you sprain your ankle or slice your flesh while trying to determine if Ginsu knives really are sharp enough to cut through aluminum cans. (They are. Oh, they are.) These loyal souls are your framily, your inner circle of confidantes, your go-to friends when the going gets tough. Naturally, you'd do the same for them.

Collected from various phases, stages, and facets of your life, each person in your framily plays an important role. (For more on the types of people in your framily, see page 51, "Typecasting: Your Framily Tree.") Together, they provide a support system that is separate and often equal to the people who gave you life, and, in turn, you are part of their support system.

Of course, the concept of framily is hardly new. Your parents probably had a few close friends who were honorary members of your family, like "Uncle" Jackie. He made appearances at every wedding, birthday, and graduation party, and even spent a few weeks living on the couch in your rec room back when you were in sixth grade. (At the time, your dad told you that Uncle Jackie just liked sleeping over because he didn't have central air-conditioning at home, but later you learned that his wife kicked him out when she realized that he loved betting on the horsies more than he loved her.)

Even though the concept of framily has been around for a long time, framilies seem much more essential today than they ever have been. Perhaps our surrogate families play a bigger role in our lives because we're getting married later than our parents and grandparents did. We're also more likely to move far away from our home bases in search of adventure and gainful employment. Anyone who has ever picked up the stakes knows how much the stakes are raised: It doesn't matter if you're in New York City or Oklahoma City, Juneau or Jacksonville. If you live in an area code where no one shares your genes, your friends are the family you choose.

You Know You're Framily When . . .

Here are some ways you can tell if she transcends "friend" and fits right into your framily.

- You can call her at 2 AM on Saturday just to say, "Holy shit! Turn on HBO! They're playing *Satisfaction*."
- She's been with you through the ups and downs—of your

bangs, that is. Of course, chances are that she's probably been with you through the joy and pains of life and all that other heavy Oprah stuff.

- You've brought her as a date to a wedding and had more fun than you did with your boyfriend at your senior prom.
- Last year, when Skippy, your family's beloved schnauzer, finally went to that big dog park in the sky, she sent you a sympathy card.
- You would trust her with your JDate.com / Match.com / meet-an-inmate.com password.
- She has sat in a waiting room with you.
- You spend hours talking—about nothing whatsoever (or at least, that's what it sounds like to your boyfriend, but you two know better).
- You have her home, cell, and work number memorized.
- You call her grandmother "Bubby."
- She knows you better than you know yourself, and she still likes you.
- You've had Thanksgiving dinner together.
- You list her as your emergency contact.
- When you leave her a voice mail, you start it off with "Hey it's me" rather than giving your name.
- She's the first to know when big things happen to you and also the first to know when the little ones do.
- You don't know what you'd do without her.

Your Family Versus Your Framily

Friends are often called your "chosen family," which implicates that they are nothing like your blood relatives. However, a closer look reveals that the dynamics, events, and people that make up your framily mirror are more similar to the family that you were born into than you would think.

	Family	**Framily**
Matriarch	Your mom	Mom Jeans (see page 59)
Annual Tradition	Drinking eggnog, listening to Bing Crosby's Christmas album, and trying to figure out how to untangle the tree lights	Drinking margaritas, smoking some trees, and trying to figure out *Vanilla Sky*
Reason for your hysterical middle-of-the-night phone call	You're broke.	You broke up with him.
TV Alter Egos	The Simpsons (plus twenty years)	Dorothy, Rose, Blanche, and Sophia (minus forty years)
Road trip	A twelve-hour hell ride to visit Colonial Williamsburg and learn boring shit like how they used to fix shoes and make butter back in the olden days	A road trip to the Anheuser-Busch brewery and learn the wonders of the Budweiser brewing process and a lengthy visit to the "sampling room"
High point	When you, your parents, and your sister kicked ass in the bocce ball tournament at your family reunion	When you and your framily kicked ass in the dart tournament at your neighborhood bar

	Family	Framily
Low point	In second grade, when your second cousin, Billy, tried to kiss you while you were playing in the fort you built in your backyard. Your mother told you to disregard the incident, because Billy was "different from the rest of us."	When your BFF's boyfriend tried to kiss you while they were on a break. The incident could've ripped your friendship apart, if she didn't decide to rip him a new asshole instead.
Black Sheep	Nicole—your first cousin who used to be Nicholas	Sarah—your first childhood friend who you had so much in common with until she had a child
Why They Give You a Headache	Your mom won't stop asking you if you're seeing someone special.	Your BFF won't stop asking you if the guy you're seeing is "special" just because he thought that Billie Holiday was a man.
Why You Love Them	You have to	How could you not?

Typecasting: Your Framily Tree

In the complex world of friendship, no one person can or should be everything to you. That is why you assemble an elite squad of highly skilled professionals who enhance your life in their own way. These are their stories. (Cue the *Law & Order* "doink doink" sound.)

- **The Childhood Best Friend:** You knew her back when talking to an imaginary friend was a sign of creativity rather than schizophrenia and napping in front of your supervisor would get you a gold star instead of a pink slip. The Childhood Best Friend was right there with you when you got your ears pierced, had your first kiss, and bought your first training bra. You and your Childhood Best Friend shared the triumphs and mortifications of growing up and somehow managed to emerge from the cocoon of braces, pimples, and acid-washed jeans as beautiful butterflies. (Well, you're a beautiful butterfly as long as you have your two cups of coffee in the morning. If not, you're more like a moth.) The two of you pinky swore that one day you'd marry twin brothers, live in huge mansions next door to each other, and have daughters who would be best friends forever too.

How to Deal: Your relationship with the Childhood Best Friend is interesting: just because she's known you the longest doesn't mean that she knows you the best, especially if you went your separate ways somewhere around middle school when she turned into a D-cup Lolita overnight and you remained a flat-chested wallflower. Regardless of your current friendship status, you have a shared history that will keep you bonded together forever—well, that and the fact that she is the only person who knows that you used to kiss your Kirk Cameron poster . . . with tongue.

- **The Best Friend:** Much like *celebrity* and *organic*, the term *best friend* has become a watered down version of its former self. Here's the thing: unlike spouses, you can totally have more than one best friend at one time (well, polygamy aside). However, many women would agree that if forced to choose, they could name the Thelma to their Louise, the Rachel to their Monica, or the Romy to their Michele. When you say to her, "Swear you won't tell anyone?" she's the only person you trust to keep her word and, likewise, you never gossip about her. All of your best memories—road trips, vacations, and crazy adventures—include her and you have no doubt that one day when both of your husbands kick it, the two of you will wreak havoc on the gated retirement community.

How to Deal: Understand that you and your best friend are as close as sisters, so a bit of bickering comes with the territory.

- **The Cruise Director:** Like holidays, death, and free food, the Cruise Director brings everybody together. Whether it's happy hour, dinner, a movie, or a vacation, she's always doing the research, sending out the invites, making the reservations, wrangling, and rallying all of your friends. She's also the only one in your framily who remembers everyone's birthdays and sends reminder e-mails to the rest of you. Sometimes you wonder what it would be like if she weren't around to extricate everyone from their very busy lives. Would your framily structure collapse like a house of playing cards or would someone else step up to steer the boat?

  How to Deal: Although the Cruise Director is a natural-born planner, make sure to thank her for her efforts, or, better yet, get off your lazy arse every once in a while and do some organizing of your own.

- **The Geographically Challenged Friend:** While long-distance relationships of the romantic variety rarely work out (remember when your high school boyfriend promised that he'd call you every day when he went away to college and absence didn't make the heart grow fonder, rather it made his eyes go wander?) long-distance friendships tend to fare much better. Sure, you have to play endless games of phone tag, converse through voice-mail messages, and look at photos from all the birthday parties, holidays, and other major life events that you couldn't be there for, but it's all worth the effort. When you and the Geographically Challenged Friend finally *are* in the same place together, it's like everything old is new again.

How to Deal: You're in luck if your Geographically Challenged Friend lives somewhere vacation worthy. (Woo-hoo! Free food and accommodations!) Even if she calls Kazakhstan home and comes to town only about as often as Haley's Comet, you can still remain close thanks to cell phones, e-mail, and IM. In fact, you can probably manage to talk to her more than your friend who lives down the block from you. Just don't forget to send her a handwritten card on her birthday.

✦ **The MVP:** Every group of friends has one. Back in high school she got a near-perfect score on her SATs and was captain of every academic and athletic team. Today, she's that same straight-A National Merit Scholar, only she wears better shoes and no longer has a perm. When she's not researching the cure for cancer, writing a screenplay, or starting up a nonprofit, she's training for a marathon and learning Japanese—you know, just for fun in her spare time. This overachiever may be the MVP of your framily, but she doesn't brag or boast about her achievements. In fact, if she wasn't such a normal, down-to-earth person with a secret passion for trashy romance novels and tabloid magazines, you'd probably hate her just a little bit.

How to Deal: Face it: you'll never be as good as the MVP. On the bright side, neither will anyone else. Instead of feeling threatened by her success, show some love for your smarty-pants pal and hope that she thanks you on the acknowledgments page of her bestselling autobiography. Plus, you can turn to her for all sorts of life advice, since the MVP has—and always will have—her shit together.

- **The Stay-at-Home Friend:** While you spend your day sitting at a desk and taking orders from your boss, the Stay-at-Home Friend spends hers sitting in a pedicure chair and taking orders from her personal trainer. She's dubiously employed (once in a blue moon, she mutters something about a "freelance" project) and she doesn't have any children (unless you count her Teacup Yorkie). What the Stay-at-Home Friend *does* have is a lifetime membership to the lucky sperm club (either that, or her husband is extremely loaded), which allows her to behave like a spoiled *heir*-head—only she doesn't. She never dangles designer purses under your nose or flaunts the fact that she can laze around all day and watch all of those awesomely bad courtroom reality shows like *Judge Judy* if she wants to. Instead, the Stay-at-Home Friend offers to wait at your place for the cable man when you get the coveted 10 AM to 4 PM time slot, she brings you chicken noodle soup and a chick flick when you're sick, and no one is more excited when you take the day off from work than she is.

  How to Deal: The Stay-at-Home Friend tests the limits of your tolerance. You believe that everyone should live and let live, but you still find it hard to keep your green-eyed monster under control when the Stay-at-Home Friend complains that she is exhausted when all she did that day was pick up the dry-cleaning and make dinner reservations. Remember, though: You don't choose your friends based on shallow things like what they do for a living or how much money they have. That's just silly. Instead, you choose them based on how pretty they are—but make sure that they aren't prettier than you.

- **The Nonsexual Life Partner:** Most prevalent in urban areas where you have to pay a small fortune for the privilege of sharing a 450-square-foot fourth-floor walk-up apartment with another human being and an innumerable number of cockroaches, the Nonsexual Life Partner often starts out as just a sane friend to share the rent with but quickly surpasses roommate status. She's more of a nag than your mother (she bangs on your door if you're not in the shower by 8 AM) and more overprotective than your father. (She insists on meeting every guy you go on a date with just in case she recognizes him from *America's Most Wanted*.) Still, a good roommate is hard to find (you should know—you've been through a string of psychotic ones), so the Nonsexual Life Partner is a comforting force in your life. In fact, you're kinda sorta dreading the day when you make enough money to live on your own or you move in with a sexual life partner. (You can guarantee that he won't know how to French braid hair as well as your Nonsexual Life Partner does.)

  How to Deal: Other than a few minor domestic disputes that led you to label your soy milk and forced her to consolidate her overflowing buffet of beauty products in the bathroom, you're happier living together than most married couples. But, just to keep things hot and sexy, crack open a bottle of red the next time you sit down to pay the bills.

✦ **The Mayor:** She rolls with a posse that would rival that of any rapper, has 350 phone numbers stored in her cell phone, and is on a first-name basis with everyone from the pharmacist to the doorman at the hottest club in town. The Mayor is a human Rolodex who makes friends wherever she goes and nothing proved that point better than her last birthday party, which had a longer line of people waiting to get in than the opening night of the last Harry Potter movie. Sometimes you can't help but wonder if you're just another entry in her address book, but the Mayor has an uncanny ability to make you feel like you're the only person in the room. Add to that the fact that she's always more than willing to exploit her vast network of connections to hook you up, whether it's telling you about a hush-hush job opening or scoring you tickets to a sold-out concert.

How to Deal: The odds that you and the Mayor will ever have a dinner together that doesn't go from a table for two to a reservation for six is slim. If you want to have her to yourself every once in a while, you just need to speak up. If she's truly framily, then she'll clear her calendar, turn off her cell, and focus all her attention on you. Just don't be surprised if she runs into at least two people she knows.

✦ **The Historian:** When you were younger, your father documented every dance recital, soccer game, and family vacation using his state-of-the-art five-pound Sony camcorder. Now that you're all grown up, the Historian has taken on the role of photo director, capturing all of your and your friends' finest moments (like when you won second place in the booty-shaking contest on Spring Break) on her credit card–sized digital camera. Unlike your other friends who promise to upload their photos and send them to you, only to accidentally erase them all the next day, the Historian takes pleasure in creating elaborate online photo albums with captions, music, and graphics within twenty-four hours of attending an event or coming home from vacation.

How to Deal: Keep your legs together, suck in your stomach, and try not to close your eyes when she takes a picture of you. And say cheese.

Friend in Focus: Mom Jeans
Your Surrogate Mother Friend

What's Her Deal? Every framily unit has a mother hen, the matriarch who keeps her chicks in line, watches protectively over them at the bar from behind her glass of white zinfandel, and always has spare tampons in her oversized purse. She's a girl gone mild: responsible and punctual (even her period is always on time), conservative (she most likely sports an Ann Taylor–meets–Ann Taylor Loft wardrobe), and reluctant to let her hair down (well, figuratively let it down, considering that she probably has a soccer mom bob). While you and your girls paint the town red, Mom Jeans, your surrogate mother friend, is perfectly content staying home and reading the latest issue of *Redbook* or spooning on the couch with Mike, her significant other, as they work their way through their Netflix queue.

Mom Jeans is far from the wildest member of your crew, but her stability adds balance to your social circle. She's also a solid friend who would give you anything, whether it was a shoulder to cry on when you find out that your boyfriend has a boyfriend or advice on matters ranging from table etiquette (she knows the purpose of every fork) to how to make a mean green bean casserole (add a dash of soy sauce for extra kick). Because Mom Jeans is such a good friend to you, you actually feel a bit of guilt when your other friends mock her love for TLC's *A Baby Story* (she can watch an entire episode without turning away in disgust during the hospital delivery scenes) or her participation in matronly hobbies, which probably include one or more of the following: scrapbooking (knitting is too punk rock for her), book club, and obsessively sending e-mail forwards that contain "just between us girls" jokes and pictures of kitties and babies.

When all is said and done, you love Mom Jeans like your family. You just wish that she would cut loose every once in while, rather than acting like your, um, actual mother.

How You Met: You and Mom Jeans began your friendship in the basement laundry room of your dorm during freshman year of college. As you struggled to separate your whites from your colors, she lent you some fabric softener and taught you how to fold T-shirts like they do at the Gap.

Symptoms of Mom Jeans

1. Ahead of Her Time: Mom Jeans was born an old—no, make that middle-aged—soul. Think Macy's and VH1 (circa the mid-nineties) rather than Victoria's Secret and MTV. Voted most likely to be the first of your friends to get married, buy a house, and spawn 2.5 children, Mom Jeans is more mature than you'll probably ever be. Even in her days as an underage college girl, the bouncers sometimes called her "ma'am" and never even looked at her fake ID (but they couldn't take their eyes off her double-D mom rack, which she always kept hidden with a minimizer bra). She had a Laura Ashley–adorned dorm room that smelled like potpourri instead of pot and was the only person who owned—and used—an iron. Today, not much has changed. Mom Jeans resides in an überadult apartment/condo/house that makes your tiny place look like a crime scene right out of *Law & Order*. And oh yeah—she has Quicken on her computer and isn't afraid to use it.

2. Identity Crisis, Averted: You spent your adolescence and young adulthood going through a host of embarrassing phases: listening to Phish, wearing patchwork pants, and slathering on patchouli in high school; at college, glow stick dancing and massaging the shoulders of total strangers at raves because you liked their "energy"; and pretending to be Carrie Bradshaw right after you graduated from school, only to later realize that you looked like an asshole/tranny hooker as you teetered around the streets wearing a tube top, sky-high stilettos, and a tutu. In stark contrast to your phases, Mom Jeans grew up unfazed. Never one to follow trends (unless they involve window treatments or kitchenware), Mom Jeans has been and always will be *herself*. Outsiders may consider this boring and vanilla (or, on the flip side, being a responsible adult), but you beg to differ. Nowadays, when every schoolteacher and accountant is hiding a scar from a belly-button ring or the fading ink of a lower back tattoo under her crisp white button-down shirt, the fact that Mom Jeans is unapologetically conventional is downright *unconventional*.

3. Monogamy Mike, Her Long-Term Significant Other: Exciting as a bowl of steamed tofu and attractive in a photo-that-comes-with-the-frame sort of way, Mom Jeans met Mike at sleepaway camp/Future Business Leaders of America/Key Club/her volunteer gig at a nursing home back when they were both in high school. They lost their virginity to each other at the appropriate age of eighteen and have been doing it (missionary style, you secretly hope) ever since. Sure, Mike isn't exactly your idea of a dream guy, but you can't help but feel a tinge of jealousy that Mom Jeans found her soul mate so early in life. Plus, deep down, you're pretty sure that they aren't just doing it missionary style. (See below.)

4. Hidden Wild Side: Perhaps you've spent too much time watching *The Ice Storm* or *Desperate Housewives* or perhaps you have too much time on your hands, but you sometimes wonder about Mom Jeans. In particular, you wonder if beneath her sweater sets and Hanes Her Way cotton briefs lies a freaky-deaky sex goddess—the type of undercover hot-to-trot suburban mama who could end up on *Real Sex 50* a few years down the road, bumping uglies with an organic farmer and his wife in a hot tub during a weekend couples Tantric retreat. It's not like you have proof of Mom Jeans's hidden wildness, but you have seen occasional cracks in her conservative veneer. (For instance, after she drank a couple of gin and tonics at her cousin's bachelorette party at Hunkmania last year, she had a little too much fun stuffing dollar bills into Ray the Hottie Handyman's tool belt.)

What's in That Big Ol' Bag of Hers?

Before the tiny Olsen twins showed up on the scene with jumbo-sized Balenciaga bags, Mom Jeans was toting her LeSportsac carryall. Filled with everything she or a small country could ever need, you always wondered what she had stashed in there. Here's a peek inside:

- Enough tampons to plug up an entire women's swim team
- Pepper spray to keep potential predators at bay (even though she lives in a suburb where the only crime consists of negligent dog walkers who leave piles of Maltipoo, Goldendoodle, and Peekapoo poop on the sidewalk)

- The latest Oprah's book club pick (she took a break from them for a while because she thought that *A Million Little Pieces* was "disgusting")
- Band-Aids, hand sanitizer, and travel-sized packages of Advil and Midol
- A sewing kit, pressed powder, a foldable hairbrush, and Binaca breath spray
- A pair of sneakers just in case her sensible Naturalizers give her trouble during her evening commute
- A couple of Netflix DVDs that need to be dropped off in the mail (*The Wedding Planner*, *Sweet Home Alabama*, and *The Sisterhood of the Traveling Pants*)
- An extra pair of L'eggs Sheer Elegance Control Tops in case she gets a run (yes she still wears pantyhose)
- *The Book of Sudoku: The Hot New Puzzle Craze*
- Her Curves membership card
- A Pocket Rocket (for when she is stuck in traffic)

Why You Love Mom Jeans: She's the friend equivalent of a Kraft dinner: warm, comforting, and cheesy in a good way.

Example: She still cries whenever she hears Sarah McLachlan's "I Will Remember You."

Why She Sometimes Irks You: Her views can sometimes make her come off as judgmental and narrow-minded. Also, like your mother, you hate to admit that she's usually right.

Example: You could swear that she made a *tsk-tsk* sound after you told her that wild story involving you, one too many tequila shots, and the hottie from accounting who seemed like a good idea at a time.

How to Be a Better Friend to Mom Jeans: Learn to keep your trap shut every once in a while and give Mom Jeans some time to vent about her problems.

How Your Friendship Will Fare: While you may not appreciate all that Mom Jeans has to offer right now, if you ever have children, she'll always be willing to carpool with you.

Where Mom Jeans Will Be in Ten Years: During the weekdays, attending PTA meetings and bake sales. On weekends, hosting "key" parties at her house while the kids are at her mom's place.

Mom Jeans and Her Dirty Little Secrets

Truth is stranger than fiction, unless, of course, we're talking about yesterday's episode of *Passions*. Mom Jeans is no Paris Hilton, or even Nicky Hilton for that matter, but as we discussed earlier, her diary contains its fair share of surprises. Even if the following dirty little secrets aren't all completely true, you can't help it if you have an overactive imagination, right? (Okay, perhaps you do need a hobby.) Here are MJ's little secrets:

- She tried pot once but it made her feel dizzy.
- She scours the real estate section—for houses in Connecticut.
- Her favorite book is *Forever* by Judy Blume, but she skips straight to the sex scenes.
- She fantasizes about getting it on with the barista at Starbucks—the girl barista.
- Her world-famous brownies come from a box of Duncan Hines mix.
- She's three months late for her six-month dental checkup.
- She used to be a card-carrying Claymate.

- She uses Summer's Eve.
- She likes back-door lovin'.

Seven Little Ways to Become a Better Framily Member

In this chapter, we've talked a lot about what how your closest friends fit into your life. When it comes down to it, though, friendship is a two-way street. So, ask not what your framily can do for you, ask what you can do for your framily. Here are some little ways you can become a better framily member.

1. Input all of your framily member's birthdays into one of your many electronic gadgets. And snail mail them a card (you know, the kind that requires a postal address and a stamp). E-cards are cute, but it's way more meaningful when you know that someone spent twenty minutes in the card aisle trying to find the perfect one just for you.
2. Make like a mother whose child has just left for college and send your Geographically Challenged Friend a care package for no reason other than you miss her.
3. Call a friend up, even if, technically, it's her turn to call you. Staying in touch with a friend shouldn't be a competition, and if you keep tabs on whose turn it is to do what, you'll lose no matter what.
4. Go on a road trip to nowhere in particular.
5. Have everyone over for dinner and by "for dinner," we mean get takeout.

6. Actually order the prints from your digital photos and make her a photo album.
7. We know that everyone is "totally crazy with work right now," but try to have standing dates with your framily members, even if it's only once a month.

Ms. Friendship Manners

Dear Ms. Friendship Manners,

I am a very blessed woman. Next year, I am going to marry the man of my dreams in a lovely outdoor ceremony on Cape Cod. I also have many close girlfriends, which is actually part of my problem. How do I choose a maid of honor without hurting anyone's feelings? I want my day to be perfect! Please tell me what to do before I say, "I do"!

Sincerely,
Frazzled in Fresno

Dear Frazzled,

Ms. Friendship Manners wishes she had your troubles. Complaining about being too popular is like complaining that one's bosoms heave too much. You say that you feel blessed, but when was the last time that you actually counted those blessings? Here is a helpful tidbit that you won't hear Ms. Friendship Manners utter very often: Not all traditions have to be followed by the book.

No one is stopping you from having several maids of honor in your bridal party or having absolutely none at all. If your girlfriends are important to you and weddings are important to them, try to involve all of them in your special day. Or, better yet, involve no one, sneak off to Sin City with your beloved, and get married in the drive-thru Tunnel of Love. This is how Ms. Friendship Manners became betrothed to her current Mr. Friendship Manners.

Sounding Off:
When the Going Gets Really Tough

Whether it's personal drama or a family matter, all of us have times when our lives resemble one of those insanely depressing episodes of *Six Feet Under.* Luckily, we have our chosen framily to lean on for love and support.

"When my dad died during college, most of my friends were completely shocked and didn't know how to react. The day I came back to school after the funeral, two of my friends came over with flowers and a couple bags of groceries, including Ben & Jerry's. It was a small gesture, but it really let me know how much they cared, even though they had no idea what to say." —Ashley, 27

"When my mom decided to leave my dad and move back to California, my mom was too depressed to really do any packing. My amazing best friend came over and helped me pack up my mom's

car and get her back where she belonged—with her family in California." —Jeanette, 29

"My friend stood by my side day and night, took every phone call, and told me all about what to expect when I found out my mom had cancer and was going to need chemotherapy because her mother went through the same thing. During the treatment, she understood every fear I had and assured me that all my scary thoughts were okay." —Tara, 23

"I had recently found out I had a benign and operable tumor that was scary nonetheless. My parents had come to visit me for a long week of tests but left that Friday. However, my two best friends from high school decided to surprise me with a girls' weekend. They drove six hours to sit around my house, make cookies, and drink lots of wine. It's hard to feel sorry for yourself when you're surrounded by good people." —Kaitlin, 26

chapter five

THE DAILY GRIND

Cubicle Comrades, Worker Bee-otches, and the Other People All Up in Your Office Space

Work is a painful reality that almost everybody has to deal with. After all, if it wasn't *work* it would be called something else, like "not work," or "sipping Prosecco on the balcony of your Italian villa."

However, there's still hope for us working stiffs and spreadsheet slaves, and it lies in our fellow cubicle comrades. People with at least three close friends at their place of employment are more likely to be extremely satisfied with their lives in general, or so says author Tom Rath in his 2006 book, *Vital Friends: The People You Can't Afford to Live Without*. Rath also found that workers who spend at least ten minutes a day watching whacked-out shit on YouTube report a higher level of job satisfaction and productivity than their non-YouTubing counterparts. (Okay, we just made that up, but you totally know it's true.)

Making friends at work is often easier said than done. Even the most Zen of offices and dreamiest of dream jobs have some sort of drama from time to time. Don't believe us? Well, here's a challenge. If you know of a workplace where everyone always multitasks, brainstorms, and crunches numbers together in perfect harmony, we'll text Santa Claus, the Easter Bunny, and the Tooth Fairy and all fly in on our magical winged unicorns for a visit to this enchanted cubicle kingdom.

More often than not, the workplace feels a lot like high school, only people get expense accounts, wear business casual attire, and have fine lines rather than pimples. And until we get replaced by robots and/or humanoids, there will always be pain with the joy in the office. Hell—even if you run your own business, you're bound to get tired of yourself at some point—unless, of course, you're Donald Trump. Work may be a four-letter word, but having friends in the office can make it the f-word: *fun*. Read on to find out how to relate to the people all up in your office space.

Real World High: The Best of the Rest of the Years of Your Life

So, we're establishing that the only thing more high school than high school itself is your office, but what if your place of employment really were a high school? Who would go to the head of the class, who would get knocked up, drop out, and move on to a life of baby's daddies, and, most important, where would you sneak out for a few detention-worthy puffs on your Marlboro Lights?

	Glamazon Jobs	White Collar Work	The Do-Good Sector	Cube Careers
The student body makeup	Slaves to fashion, entertainment, and any other glam industry that mistakes bipolar and histrionic personality disorders for "genius"	Investment bankers, hedge fund women, corporate lawyers, and all jobs that reek of Reaganomics	Non-profit employees, social workers, professional tree huggers, and other giving souls	Middle management, insurance adjusters, widget salespeople, and desk-jockey professions that lead to carpel tunnel syndrome
Think . . .	*Mean Girls* meets *The Devil Wears Prada*	*Risky Business* meets *Wall Street*	*Dazed and Confused* meets *An Inconvenient Truth*	*Better Off Dead* meets *Office Space*
Uniform	Anything with a designer label in a size 2 on top and Manolos, Choos, or Louboutins on the bottom	Brooks Brothers for now; custom tailoring later	Eco-friendly fashion made from smokeable fabrics	Trousers, button-downs, cardigans, and pumps for the office; sneakers for the commute
Mascot	André Leon Talley	Patrick Bateman	Al Gore	Clippit, the Microsoft Word Office Assistant
School colors	Whatever is the "new black"	Amex Platinum	Green	Banana Republic's fall color palette
Fight song	"Supermodel (You Better Work)" by RuPaul	"It's All About the Benjamins" by Diddy, featuring Notorious B.I.G. and Lil' Kim	"Imagine" by John Lennon	"Working for the Weekend" by Loverboy

	Glamazon Jobs	**White Collar Work**	**The Do-Good Sector**	**Cube Careers**
Class prank	Ordering the boss a latte with whole milk instead of skim	Sending an office-wide e-mail with the subject line, "Insider Trading Investigation"	Signing the staff up for a Young Republican fund-raiser	Sneaking a slide of Mr. Hankey the Christmas Poo into the marketing department's holiday season Powerpoint presentation
Extracurricular activities	Not eating	Sexually harassing the female employees	Raging against the machine	Checking job postings on monster.com
Yearbook quote	"Whoever said orange was the new pink was seriously disturbed."	"Greed is good."	"Meat is murder."	"Life moves pretty fast. If you don't stop to look around once in a while, you could miss it."
Cafeteria favorite	Bottled water	Lunch is for pussies	Tofutti snacks	Taco Tuesdays!
Weekend hangout(s)	The four B's: Barneys, Bloomies, Bergdorfs, and Bendels	With the double-D's in the Champagne room at Scores	The food co-op	Pottery Barn, Crate and Barrel, and Home Depot
Smoke break	Virginia Slims in the fashion closet	Cubans in the conference room	Bong hits at 4:20 in the bathroom	The parking lot
How you spent your summer vacation	Summering	Coked up	Building houses in some third world country	Coaching Little League
How to be voted most popular	Declare skinny jeans "so last year"	Bring back the all-you-can-eat shrimp cocktail table at the holiday office party	Grow your own green	Fix the paper misfeed in the copy machine

Typecasting: The People All Up in Your Office Space

If you were to add up all the hours you spend at work in one year and compare that number to the amount of time you spend doing more enjoyable things such as, um, not working, you'd be really depressed, so don't even bother. Even if you're one the lucky few who actually knows the color of your parachute, you will still benefit from befriending the people who share your cube space. Here are some common office-friendly archetypes and how you can relate to each of them:

- **The Office Us Weekly:** The Office *Us Weekly* is your go-to girl when you want to know who's doing what and who's doing it with whom in your cubicle kingdom. Never one to discriminate, she's got dirt on everyone from the CEO and other Very Important People at the top of the corporate ladder all the way down to the lowest rungs, where the temps and interns toil. A whiz at multitasking, the Office *Us Weekly* possesses the ability to collect and disseminate gossip at lightning speed, distort facts, and fabricate sources, all while simultaneously doing expense reports. She's also got a knack for getting people to spill their dirty little secrets. But remember, you didn't hear it from her.

  How to Deal: The Office *Us Weekly* is just like her namesake magazine: a guilty pleasure that isn't always the most reliable or trustworthy of sources. Befriend her if you want some cheap entertainment, but buyer beware: while you love how she can make your office sound as exciting as a soap opera, resist the urge to talk-trash about your coworkers in her presence. Also, steer clear of the Office *Us Weekly* if you've had a couple of margaritas at happy hour—unless you want everyone at your place of employment to know that you were canoodling with Dan from accounts payable at Bennigan's last week.

✦ **The Work Husband:** He's smart, funny, and easy to talk to, but it's not like you want to marry him or anything. He's your Work Husband—your confidante Monday through Friday, from 9 AM to 5 PM. While you and your Work Husband have zero romantic interest in each other, you feel slightly guilty that you spend about as much time with him as you do with your actual boyfriend. On the other hand, if you've ever been cornered at a dinner party by someone who thinks that people actually want to hear all about the fascinating world of middle management, you already understand the importance of your Work Husband. He's your career counselor. You can bitch and moan to him about office stuff and get it out of your system by the time you log off of Windows for the day. This frees up your mind for more meaningful post-work conversation topics, like, is so-and-so starlet pregnant or just bloated?

How to Deal: When it comes to your Work Husband, it's all good as long as your friendship stays relatively professional. Here are some signs that things between the two of you are getting a little too close for comfort: 1. You spend more time confiding in him during non–work hours. 2. You divulge way too many details about your personal relationships. 3. You bang.

✦ **The Corporate Nonconformist:** Just because she's working for the man doesn't mean that she has to act like it. With her dreams of becoming an artist, musician, or Sylvia Plath (minus the whole offing-herself-in-an-oven thing) neatly tucked away in a drawer next to her bong and her journal, the Corporate Nonconformist still finds little ways to rage against the machine despite the fact that she has resigned herself to a life among the cubicles. Her wardrobe leans more toward Hot Topic than J. Crew, her lunches are of the liquid variety, and she wears headphones and listens to loud, angry music as she types away at her computer—which is banned per company policy. Even though she likes to act out like a petulant teenager, none of her superiors seem to mind. In fact, the Corporate Nonconformist is a lot like that cool outsider from high school who wore black nail polish (this was before Chanel called it "Black Satin" and sold it for thirty-plus dollars a bottle), dated a hot older guy who drove a muscle car, played drums in an all-girl punk band, and was secretly a mega-genius.

How to Deal: A friendship with the Corporate Nonconformist can help show you that you don't have to become a khaki-clad robot like the rest of them. However, be wary if her influence extends into rebel-without-a-cause territory. It's one thing to swipe a few extra Post-it notes, but once she convinces you to use the corporate account to overnight a package of homemade brownies to your boyfriend who is studying the native tribes of Zimbabwe, you risk a rather unpleasant meeting with HR. Besides, black nail polish is *so* out this season.

- **The Workplace Bicycle:** The Workplace Bicycle is a good time—in fact, she's such a good time that she's done the

Tour de France with all of the eligible bachelors in your office (and even some of them in your Stamford, Connecticut, branch). While you think she's a nice person, you fear getting too close to her, lest you become a ho by association.

How to Deal: When it comes to the Workplace Bicycle, don't play for both teams (and no, we don't mean playing for both teams in the way that the Office *Us Weekly* claimed she did after the office holiday party in 2005). In other words, don't act like a friend to her face and then turn around and spread nasty gossip behind her back to your coworkers. That stuff will keep coming back to burn you, much like the sore on her lip that the Workplace Bicycle allegedly caught from Tom in sales. You don't want to get a reputation—as an office mean girl.

- **The Motivational Speaker:** More upbeat than Kelly Ripa on uppers, the Motivational Speaker either believes in the power of positive thinking or is positively crazy. Regardless of her mental state, you marvel at her ability to maintain a sunny outlook at the office even on those days when the work seems never ending and the red tape feels like it's long enough to circumvent the globe. Every time you walk by the Motivational Speaker's desk (where she'll always greet you with a Stepford Wife smile and a Miss America wave), you can't help but wonder if she's got a big old bottle of happy pills and a loaded Smith & Wesson locked in the filing cabinet below her joke-a-day calendar.

  How to Deal: Believe it or not, some people are generally happy with their jobs. Even more unbelievable, some people are just happy in general. While you don't need to pee sunshine and poop rainbows, thinking good thoughts never hurt a person (or, at least, that's what *The Secret* tells us). Buddy up to the Motivational Speaker. When you're feeling burned out, a pep talk from her can help put everything into perspective and stop you from thinking so many negative thoughts. Being nice to her also has an added perk: on that fateful day when she finally goes completely postal, perhaps she'll let you flee the building unharmed before she starts shootin' up the place.

- **The Relic:** She's been with your company since they used carbon paper and overhead projectors and she vividly remembers when employees smoked cigarettes at their desks and could retire before the age of 75. If you want something done yesterday, the Relic is definitely not the person to rely on, considering she still has trouble opening e-mail attachments and prefers to sort and staple documents by hand rather than figure out how to use the collate function on the copier. Even though she is friendly with everyone in your office from the maintenance guy to the CEO, no one knows how old she is (the general consensus is that her age falls somewhere between 60 and 160), nor do they know what she actually does all day. (There's a theory that she was fired back in 1986, but just keeps coming into the office, anyway.)

  How to Deal: Before you write off the Relic as being the equivalent of the pillow-sized maxi pads in the bathroom dispenser (old-fashioned and useless, not to mention unwieldy), keep in mind that she has seen many employees who are just like you come and go, so she might actually know a thing or two about the inner workings of your company. Make it a point to have lunch with the Relic once a month and take in her wisdom. At the very least, she might tell you where the secret stash of letter-sized manila folders is hidden. (Who uses the legal ones anyway?)

- **The Worker Bee-otch:** If you thought that excessive amounts of backstabbing, ass-kissing, and scheming were reserved for the set of *Desperate Housewives,* then you have yet to get tangled up in the Worker Bee-otch's web of bitchery and deceit. This brand of office *frenemy* has three identifying characteristics: a perma-smirk, the Teflon-like ability to avoid doing any actual work, and a raging case of *friendship schizophrenia.* When she asks you for "a teeny tiny favor," she's sweeter than the three Splenda packets in your coffee. Then, before the ink is even dry on the fifteen-page Excel document you spent hours working on for her, she turns around and outs you for having a forbidden space heater under your desk. Damn her!

  How to Deal: You might think that the best way to handle the Worker Bee-otch is by maintaining a safe distance. However, the cooler you act toward her the more likely she is to turn the heat up on your ass. Why else do you think your coworkers, who, despite the Worker Bee-otch's reputation, remain pleasant and are even nice to her? It's not because they *don't* know what she's capable of.

Friend in Focus: Your Office BFF

What's Her Deal: She's so *not* like a sister to you. She doesn't know about that one time in first grade when you peed your pants during gym class or how you got your heart broken on Valentine's Day 1999 by some guy named Mitch who went to raves and had a pierced eyebrow. Hell, she probably doesn't even know your middle name. It's all fine by you, though, because she's your Office BFF, the one who keeps you sane when the daily grind starts grinding you down. While she might not be privy to all of your dirty little secrets, she's still an invaluable part of your social stratosphere. She's your sounding board, your boardroom backup, and a welcome dose of reality when you find yourself slipping into a Microsoft Excel–induced catatonic state. But, above all, she's a friend. Without your Office BFF, 9 to 5 would feel more like an eternity and Wednesday night happy hour would be a lot less happy.

How You Meet: The two of you make eye contact from across the conference table during a sexual harassment awareness seminar. When the word *fondle* appears on-screen during the PowerPoint presentation, you both suppress a fit of giggles until your abs ache like you've just done a total core workout. After trying really hard to act mature, you and your new partner in crime finally lose it when the stone-cold serious presenter drops the phrase "thinking outside the box" into her discussion about inappropriate relations in the workplace. (He he—she said *box*.) Your outburst elicits a room full of dirty looks, but it also gives birth to a friendship that will last forever—or at least until your jobs get outsourced to India.

Symptoms of Your Office BFF

1. It's Nothing Personal: Because you spend forty-plus hours per week with your Office BFF (which is exponentially more time than you spend with all of your other friends) you feel comfortable sharing rather intimate information with each other. For example, she knows that when you go number two at work it has to be in the third stall. However, despite the regular exchange of T.M.I., some important facts—like what she got on her SATs, her astrological sign, and what her parents do for a living—remain a mystery. Maybe it's because of your lack of history or because you're too busy speculating about the executive assistant's sexual orientation, but something prevents the two of you from swimming in the deep end of the friendship pool.

2. Cubicle Catharsis: You and your Office BFF spend hours ruminating about the injustices and inner workings of your office—topics that typically bore your nonwork friends to tears. Your conversations with her are a lot like an *America's Next Top Model* marathon: Sure, you've seen all the episodes before, but watching them over and over again is strangely comforting.

You and your Office BFF typically start the day off with lattes and some light chitchat about your workloads. At lunchtime, you sequester yourselves at the back table in the cafeteria where you gossip about your boss's tragic fashion sense. (Nude hose?! Does she think she's in a dance recital or something?) But happy hour is where the real Page Six–quality gossip happens and the two of you share rumors about hirings, firings, affairs, and drama over the sweet combination of light beer and jalapeño poppers.

3. Fear of Abandonment: Every time you throw yourself across her desk, lament about the *deadendedness* of your job, and vow to walk out of this evil empire and do some honest work like serving up some fries and extra value meals, your Office BFF begs you not to quit. You feel the same way. If she ever left, who would keep her drawer stocked with tampons because you're on the same period cycle or help you change the toner in the copy machine for the hundredth time? One evening, after a couple of postwork glasses of pinot noir, the two of you even go so far as to make a vow to quit at the end of the year together. (You even signed your names in eyeliner on a cocktail napkin.) However, in a shocking turn of events, your Office BFF ends up leaving you behind to go to law school in Chicago just a month after you forged your work-suicide pact. You pretend that you're happy for her, but deep down, you feel a bit betrayed. (Actually, you're more jealous than betrayed because she beat you to the punch.)

4. Separate Worlds: It's not that your Office BFF wouldn't get along with your nonwork friends. It's just that your friendship with her exists in a vacuum and when you take it into the real world, things can get a bit awkward. For instance, remember that one time at your birthday party when your Office BFF stood in the corner and talked only to your other coworkers even though you've told her so many great things about your friends? (Okay, so maybe you told her about your one friend's habit of getting wasted and throwing drinks on strangers.) After that incident you realized that it's easier to treat her like a new boyfriend whom you don't want to introduce to your family for fear that he'll run away screaming.

Why You Love Your Office BFF: She's a team player.

Example: When you spilled Diet Coke on your keyboard for the third time this month and were freaking out that you were going to have to pay for a new one out of your own pocket, your Office BFF agreed to go out on a date with Larry the IT guy, who has a massive crush on her. You're not sure what happened that night but the next morning there was a brand-new keyboard on your desk.

Why She Irks You: She is nice to everyone.

Example: Even though she's clearly on your side after you have a passive aggressive e-mail fight with another coworker, she still says hi to her in the bathroom. Traitor.

How Your Friendship Will Fare: Unless you really make the effort to stay in touch, your affair might end as soon as you finish your exit interview with HR.

Where She'll Be in Ten Years: How the hell should you know? Once she ditched working 9 to 5 for the life of a law student, the two of you lost touch. Come to think of it, you did hear something about her marrying Larry the IT guy last summer.

Caution Signals: What You Don't Want in an Office BFF

So, what happens when your Office BFF hands in her resignation letter and leaves you behind in her dust? You go on with your life and attempt to find someone else who will make work that much more fun. Here are some caution signals that will help you realize early on that she probably isn't going to be your corporate soul mate.

1. She's addicted to speakerphone.
2. She has any of the following in her cube: a Successories poster, stuffed animals, and/or a jar filled with old-lady, sugar-free hard candies.
3. She's never heard of *Office Space*.
4. She has a headset receiver and isn't afraid to use it.
5. She tries to engage you in Jesus talk at work.
6. She proudly wears/carries/uses the company logo–emblazoned T-shirt/tote bag/umbrella that you were all given last year in lieu of a holiday bonus, rather than stashing it under her bed, regifting it, or burning it like everyone else did.
7. She breezes by your desk and says things like "Happy Monday!" and "Someone needs to turn that frown upside down!"
8. She thinks it's wrong to steal the free tampons in the ladies' room.
9. She uses a mug with a picture of her kids on it.
10. She brings in cupcakes for the boss's birthday.

Famous Work Friends:
An Analysis

Ever notice how some well-known big and small screen coworker BFFs sound like frenemies more than friends? Sure, entertainment value and ratings are mostly to blame for the biting put-downs and the witty banter, but their unique relationships also got us thinking. You can get so close to a coworker that they start to feel like family. As a result, your interactions resemble that of siblings who are brutally honest and can't resist a cheap shot. Here, some memorable on-screen exchanges that prove our theory:

Grace Adler and Karen Walker (Will & Grace)

Karen: Honey, you're being so spiteful and vindictive.

Grace: Compliments? This early in the day?

Meredith Grey and Cristina Yang (Grey's Anatomy)

Cristina: Meredith, I have a thing . . . news.

Meredith: You're not pregnant again, are you? Because I can't handle the extra months of bitchiness.

Simon Cowell and Paula Abdul (American Idol)

Simon: I still don't understand a single word you say Paula.

Paula: Then I'm doing my job.

Amanda Tanen and Marc St. James (Ugly Betty)

Amanda: You told me my head was too big for my neck.

Marc: It was constructive criticism.

Andy Sachs and Nigel (The Devil Wears Prada)

Andy Sachs: Well, I'm a six. . . .

Nigel: Which is the new fourteen.

Playing Nice: How to Make Friends in Your Place of Employment

If you're starting a new job or are in need of some pleasant distractions at your 9 to 5, there are a few foolproof ways you can make new friends.

- Bring food to share. People (literally) eat that shit up. Hell, it can even be a box of Dunkin' Donuts Munchkins. Extra brownie points if you made those brownies yourself. (Here's a helpful hint, though: Make sure to transfer the cookies from the Entenmann's box into some Tupperware containers before you try to convince everyone that you baked them with your own two hands.)
- Join the office softball team or, if you were the kid who was always picked last in gym class, fake a chronic knee injury, watch from the sidelines, and join in the action at the bar after the game.
- You don't have to act like a flight attendant, but a smile and a nod goes a long way. Say "hi" to coworkers when you pass their cubes on the way to the can. Remember to use common sense, though, and don't stand at the bathroom sink and try to converse with a fellow worker as she hovers over the toilet seat on the other side of the stall door.
- Take the initiative and invite your fellow workers to join you for lunch, postwork drinks or eats, or anything really, that gives you the chance to get away from the office, get to know one another better, and talk about your coworkers who aren't there with you.
- Part of making new friends is being a good friend. Make

the effort to actually remember little details about your coworkers or, at the very least, learn their names. They'll appreciate the effort. If you have a problem matching faces to names, use little tricks to pump up your short-term memory. Try associating the first letter of someone's first name with something about that person that begins with the same letter. For example: *S*teve *s*tares at your boobs. *E*llen has *e*ighties hair. *J*ill has *j*unk in the trunk.

Lunch Is a Battlefield

The midday meal is a time when you and your Office BFF can relax and unwind and by "relax and unwind," we mean "stuff your faces and bitch about your boss behind her back." Following the mantra that "you are what you eat," below are some observations from the break room about your fellow cubicle slaves and their lunch choices:

- **A Lean Cuisine and a Diet Coke:** I enjoy dressing my cat in clothing, crocheting large afghans, and watching made-for-TV movies.
- **Make-your-own salad with romaine lettuce, shredded carrots, cucumbers, tomatoes, grilled chicken, and low-fat dressing on the side:** I'm about as intriguing as an episode of *7th Heaven*.
- **Last night's take-out leftovers:** I store shoes in my oven, keep nail polish and olives in my fridge, and would give anything to go on a date instead of watching *Designing Women* reruns with my roommate.

- **Super-sized burger (with extra-special sauce), fries, and a large Mountain Dew:** I eat my emotions.
- **Black coffee and a cigarette:** I get all the sustenance I need by sucking the blood and the youth from nubile, wide-eyed junior account execs such as yourself.
- **Long, überexpensive lunches with "clients":** I make twice as much as you do, yet I do half the amount of work. Sucka.
- **Three martinis:** I hate my husband and am sleeping with my kickboxing instructor, Fernando.

Friends in High Places: The People in Your Office You Don't Want to Piss Off

We've established that having a few friends in your office (or at least people you can waste time with) will make coming to work more pleasant. It's also worth mentioning that you should make an effort to befriend everyone you encounter from 9 to 5. First of all, it's polite to know the names of the people you see every day, but, more important, it pays to befriend those who have the power to make your job a hell of a lot easier.

1. **The main IT geek:** The only person more important than your boss is the one who has the password to your computer and the ability to pull up any questionable keywords in your Internet search history. Find out what his or her favorite snack food is and stock up on it. You'll need it to bribe him or her when you accidentally send the head of your company an e-mail that describes just how well your date went last night.
2. **Cafeteria workers:** Did you know that a snot rocket can

be launched into your turkey burger so quickly that your eyes can't even detect it? Okay, not really, but just in case, make nice with anyone who prepares and serves your food. Not only will your friendly café worker give you an extra pickle with your sandwich, but he or she is the only one who can pull a few strings and get them to start serving Cherry Coke, rather than Wild Cherry Pepsi.

3. Assistants: The devil may wear Prada, but her assistant is the one who really holds the keys to the kingdom. Become chummy with her and she'll squeeze you in for a meeting, make sure your memo makes it to the top of the in-box, and warn you when the boss catches an earlier flight back and will be making a surprise cameo in the office. And if you can get her drunk enough at happy hour she just might tell you what year your boss was really born (that eye job isn't fooling anyone).

4. Interns: The peons of your office may not seem like they have much to offer you, but consider this: today's lowly bottom-feeders are tomorrow's assistants. (Also, you were yesterday's intern.) Plus, being that the higher-ups use them as full-time errand runners, interns are usually privy to some fascinating information, such as which supervisor gets her freakishly perky demeanor from a cocktail of pharmaceuticals and who has a rather loose definition of a "work expense."

5. The office manager: Do we really have to tell you why it's good to be in with the person whose job includes approving raises, allotting vacation days, hirings, firings, and settling coworker disputes?

6. The mail room peeps: You know the mail room's strict five o'clock deadline for next-day delivery? Well, it's actually quite flexible if you know the right people. Plus, if you're really nice to the guys and gals down there (think baked goods and lots of them), they'll keep your habit of sending out personal packages on the company's dime just between you and them.

7. The cleanup crew: Everyone assumes that your heavy workload is the reason you always stay late at work—that is, everyone but the janitorial staff who consistently see you updating your résumé on your work computer when everyone else is long gone. Get the girls in the office to stop flushing paper towels and feminine products down the toilet and your after-hours activities will remain a secret, as will any incriminating evidence.

8. Security personnel: When most people lose their office ID they have to go through a lengthy process at the security desk. Luckily, you're not most people, because you shoot the shit with the security guard every morning. So when your little plastic card goes missing, he hooks you up with a new one in minutes and lets you retake the picture until you get one that doesn't make you look like Sloth from *The Goonies*.

chapter six

FRENEMIES

The Users, Losers, and Abusers Who You Need to De-MySpace Right Now

She's the Veronica to your Betty, the Tom to your Jerry, and the Heather #1 to your Heather #2. She invites you shopping when your credit card is maxed out, brings you cupcakes when you're trying to cut back on calories, and brags about her fabulous, very important job when you're barely staying afloat in the corporate shark tank. Basically, she takes sick pleasure in your pain.

On the flip side, she might be the type of person who (consciously or subconsciously) uses less obvious tactics to cut you down to size. Perhaps she's a part-time pal who comes around only after her boyfriend dumps her or she gets wind of your killer summer beach rental. Or she could possess *Single White Female* tendencies and act crazy jealous whenever you do anything in life that doesn't include her.

It doesn't really matter what she is—underminer, user, clinger, backstabber, or simply clueless. (We can also think of some other names, but we've started a "swear" jar and would like to hold on to our money.) The only thing that matters is what she *isn't*: a real friend. Instead, she's an honest-to-goodness frenemy: part friend and part enemy, part passive and part aggressive. She's a shapeshifter, going from sweet to sour in the matter of a happy hour and she often leaves you with the same headache you get after having one too many two-for-one apple martinis.

So, here's the big question: You wouldn't tolerate this kind of bad behavior in a boyfriend, so how come your frenemy is granted a get-out-of-jail-free card? Well, this isn't a multiple-choice test, but we have a few possible answers as to why you let her hurt you so badly: 1. Because you're a glutton for punishment or you secretly like the drama. 2. Because you believe the good in her outweighs the bad. 3. Because you feel guilty about cutting a friend loose. 4. Because you're afraid to tell her how you really feel.

We're here to say that life is too short to waste on negative people. (Hell, you barely have enough time to spend with the ones you love.) If you are truly plagued with a toxic frenemy, it's time to—pardon the allusions to the potty—drop a deuce or get off the pot. You need to determine if a sorta friendship can be saved or if it needs to be pulled off life support.

Of course, we're not talking about abandoning a real friend who is going through a rough patch (because in that case the frenemy might be *you*). This is about standing up for yourself, rather than lying down on the ground and letting her step all over you in her spiky stilettos, and if you're into that type of thing, you need to put down this book and look for some Internet chat rooms or something.

Besides, if you do nothing but complain about a frenemy behind her back, there's another reason why she treats you like she does: because you let her.

It's Not Me, It's You: The Frenemy's Favorite Sayings

You were always a believer of your mother's "sticks and stones" mantra—that is, until you encountered your frenemy. She doles out compliments with a backhand that would make Maria Sharapova jealous and always manages to say something that gets under your skin. Here are some of her more memorable lines:

- You look tired.
- I'm sorry you feel that way.
- You're going to eat *all* of that?
- Well, he's not exactly my type, but you might like him.
- What did you do to your hair?
- I'll just have a salad with balsamic vinegar on the side.
- Those shoes are so . . . you.
- Your nose/weight/teeth/feet/hair gives you character.
- It's okay. Some of us just aren't "relationship" people.
- Things like that just don't bother me.
- I was at the gym all night.
- Now, don't take this the wrong way but . . . [insert something that you can't help but take the wrong way].
- The movie has subtitles, so you might not get it.
- Your ex-boyfriend's new girlfriend is sooo pretty.

Typecasting: Know Thine Frenemies

If you're one of those people who read celebrity tabloids and watch a lot of television, then you probably think all frenemies are anorexic blondes who wear designer clothes. However, you'll be surprised to discover so-called friends comes in all shapes, sizes, and hair colors. But the one characteristic that they all share is a dependence on theatrics. For the best performance in a drama, the nominees are . . .

- **The Ditcher:** When she's between boyfriends, the Ditcher is all over you like tattoos on Amy Winehouse. Suffering from a bizarre form of mania brought on by her single status, she wants to hang out 24/7 and be involved in an intense type of friendship that usually exists only between twelve-year-olds who wear best friend necklaces. However, as soon as a new man enters her life, the Ditcher drops off the face of the Earth, only to resurface months later via a series of hysterical voice mails that she left you at 2:01, 2:10, and 2:18 on a Wednesday morning because he told her that he wants to take a break and why aren't you picking up? She runs hot and cold, and you're getting tired of her bipolar behavior.

  How to Deal: Every romantic relationship goes through a honeymoon phase where both lovey-dovey parties involved voluntarily isolate themselves from the rest of the group and retreat to their own personal love shack. You get it. In fact, you've probably done it before. Then, after a bit of time passes and said couple realizes that life isn't one long De Beers commercial, they reintroduce themselves to society. Either the Ditcher lacks the ability to find balance in her life or she lets a-holes, jerks, and tools consume her entire being. On the frenemy scale, the Ditcher's offensiveness depends on the extent of her ditching. For instance, despite her romantically induced flightiness, does she still manage to be by your side when the big things happen in your life? If she couldn't even find the time to pay her condolences when your beloved nana passed away, get off this seesaw friendship when the Ditcher is on top and let her crash down on her sorry ass.

- **The Queen Me:** The Queen Me is so in touch with her feelings that she can't be bothered with anyone else's. Her likes: herself. Her dislikes: everything else. When you first meet the Queen Me, she tricks you into thinking that she cares about others, but in time, you realize that you'll always be sitting in the back row of the audience for her one-woman show. (For example, when the two of you went out for burritos and margaritas last week, the Queen Me seemed like she was listening intently as you vented about a particularly hellish week at work, but she was actually just gazing at her reflection in a nearby window.)

  How to Deal: While the Queen Me isn't evil or anything, you need to understand that she's not the type of friend who will help move your stuff into a new apartment or sit with you in any sort of waiting room. If you can deal with having someone in your life that you can't really depend on, more power to you. If not, it may be time to peacefully move on and give the Queen Me what she really wants: more time with herself.

- **The Ike Turner:** Like an abusive boyfriend straight out of a Lifetime movie (and played by Richard Grieco), the Ike Turner thinks she owns you or something. On one hand, she's an incredibly loyal friend. On the other, she gets jealous of anything or anyone who cuts into your "together" time, which includes just about everything and everyone. You feel torn: you don't want her out of your life, but you can't keep living like you're Julia Roberts in *Sleeping with the Enemy*.

How to Deal: Since the Ike Turner is loyal, you need to talk to her about taking it down a notch. Kindly explain that just because you have to do things like work, sleep, and shower doesn't mean that you're blowing her off. After your little talk, if the Ike Turner still isn't getting it, hide out in a safe place with a relative or close friend, learn jujitsu, and then go all *Crouching Tiger, Hidden Dragon* on her ass.

- **The Enabler:** The Enabler is supportive and encouraging—of the person you don't want to become. Whether your poison is shopping, sweets, bad boys, or illicit substances, she has this amazing ability to get you to buy, eat, smoke, sleep with, snort, or drink the things that hurt you good. (C'mon. Everybody's doing it!) You've had fun times together, but hanging out with the Enabler is increasingly bad for your health.

  How to Deal: If your Enabler can't respect the fact that you are on a budget/diet/bad-boy boycott/twelve-step program, tell her that you've picked up a new habit that you hope she can enable: staying the fuck away from her.

- **The Gossip:** Whatever you tell the Gossip goes in one ear and out to the entire world. She holds on to secrets like Pamela Anderson holds on to her dignity. You'd like to think that her slipups are the result of some rare form of Tourette's, but deep down you know that the Gossip's motivations for spilling the beans are much more sinister. She just wants to make herself look better than you, which ain't happening without a full makeover and a few months' of Pilates classes. (Okay, that was petty and low, but so was the time that she accidentally-on-purpose told your crush that you clogged the toilet at her house.)

How to Deal: You have two choices: either be a big girl and cut off contact with your loose-lipped frenemy or act like it's high school all over again, feed her gossipy "exclusives" about your other frenemies (which may or may not be true), and watch the drama unfold. However, here's a warning: if you choose to go the high school route, expect to get into a fight in the schoolyard at 3:05 sharp.

- **The Unfriendly Competition:** Anything you can do she can do better. You get highlights? She goes platinum blond. You get promoted to a middle manager at work? She gets promoted to upper management. You get a new boyfriend? She gets two. Much like there's good stress and bad stress, there's also productive and destructive competition. The Unfriendly Competition obviously serves up a dose of the latter. Rather than pushing you to succeed, she leaves you feeling bitter and envious of her successes and guilty that you are stooping to her childish level.

  How to Deal: In many cases, the Unfriendly Competition is an unavoidable frenemy who is woven into the fabric of your professional life. While you can't change her behavior, you can alter how you react to it. Remember this commandment for dealing with frenemies (which also applies to friends): Thou shall not covet her life. Next time you feel the urge to one-up her or snap back at one of the many digs she makes (*You don't look well. Are you sick?*) do absolutely nothing at all. Without your negativity to fuel her, she won't know what to do and will spin round and round without actually going anywhere, much like a record or a hamster in a wheel.

- **The Black Hole:** Unfortunately, the Black Hole isn't in a galaxy far, far away. She's part of your social stratosphere, sucking out the light, optimism, and good vibes from anyone who gets too close to her orbit. If she had a slogan it would be "woe is me"; her theme song would be one long, drawn-out sigh. You've tried over and over again to be a good friend to this negative Nancy, but you're finding it hard to believe that so many bad things can happen to one person. Plus, she finds the bad in everything and everyone. You can't even have a simple phone conversation with her that doesn't leave you feeling physically and emotionally drained, like you've just watched *Old Yeller*.

  How to Deal: Dealing with the Black Hole can be tough because she appeals to your inner handywoman. You expend a lot of energy trying to fix her and make her happy, but only the Black Hole can make herself see the light. (Actually, the right medication and extensive therapy might also do the trick.) Offer her your support—and your shrink's phone number.
- **The User:** Like her namesake implies, the User will befriend anyone who can contribute to a cause that is close to her heart—herself—and give nothing back in return. For example, when she heard that you rented a beach house for the summer, she was your best friend from Memorial Day to Labor Day, and just days after you accepted a job with a clothing company, she asked you about the friends and family discount. Of course, whenever you ask the User for

the smallest of favors, she gives you a look of horror, like you just kicked a puppy or something.

How to Deal: The key to maintaining your sanity in this frenemy-ship depends on your willingness to accept that her loyalty will last only as long as the concert you were able to score her tickets for. Actually, do yourself a favor and don't return her phone call the next time Justin Timberlake/Gwen Stefani/the White Stripes/Hall & Oates are in town and she wants you to "work your connections."

- **The Politician:** On paper, the Politician seems like she'd make an ideal friend. She's diplomatic, agreeable, and nonconfrontational. However, in reality she suffers from the disease to please, an affliction that causes her to talk out of both sides of her mouth and prevents her from forming a solid opinion on everything from her favorite color to the death penalty. It would seem that the only person the Politician would bother is herself, however her dependency on others for guidance and her constant flip-flopping makes it nearly impossible to have anything but a surface friendship with her. Also, she has a problem saying no to anything or anyone, which makes her flaky and hard to depend on.

  How to Deal: Force the Politician to take a stance and stick with it—it's for her own good. Start out with something simple like what movie she wants to see (not what movie she thinks you want to see) then move on to bigger issues, such as her feelings on low-fat fro-yo versus fat-free.

Frenemy in Focus: Putting the Fun in Dysfunctional—Your Psycho Friend

What's Her Deal? Whether it's the hormones in her birth control pills (when she remembers to take them), middle-child syndrome, or just a run-of-the-mill serotonin deficiency, your psycho friend is more unpredictable than Paula Abdul on a live broadcast. She's the one on *The Real World* who gets a slow-mo montage as she consumes alcohol at an alarming rate and after the commercial break tries to sleep with the hot-yet-sensitive-yet-dumb-as-a-bag-of-rocks frat guy. When he rejects her sloppy, Smirnoff Ice–soaked advances, she stumbles upstairs and cries to the hot gay roommate that no one understands her. Then she tries to make out with *him*. When he turns her down, she dials up her boyfriend from back home in Gary, Indiana, tells him that she loves him, and then she runs outside, pees in the street, and gets carted away by the police for an evening of detox in the drunk tank. And that's just the first episode of the season.

Sure, your psycho friend has her share of problems, but you know her well enough to see the light through her tunnel of dysfunction. For starters she has a lot of loyalty to you, like that one time when she launched a piece of Orbit Bubblemint into a girl's hair because she accidentally bumped into you at a bar. The psycho also has an unparalleled ability to turn an otherwise dull situation—whether it's a bris or a diversity training seminar at work—into something way more exciting. Yet, despite these redeeming qualities, she's becoming the friend equivalent of *The O.C.*—entertaining at first, but just too much over-the-top drama as the years go by. And frankly, you're scared to see what'll happen in the series finale.

How You Met: You met at Mountain Lake Day Camp the summer before your senior year in high school, where the two of you worked as counselors. She stole Fudgsicles from the snack shack and smoked cigarettes on the nature trail. You loved her spontaneity and her chutzpah. For eight weeks, you felt like Liv and Alicia in Aerosmith's "Crazy" video.

Symptoms of the Psycho

1. Liar, Liar, Pants on Fire: Much like your four-year-old niece likes to go on and on about the monsters under her bed and the fairies in her closet, the Psycho also has a lively imagination. Luckily, you learned early on to disregard about 75 percent of what comes out of her mouth. (You stopped believing her stories during senior year of high school, when she swore up and down that she could get you tickets to the sold-out K-Rock-a-thon because her second cousin was the drummer for Third Eye Blind. You waited for this supposed cousin outside of the Coliseum for three hours and finally gave up and went to Denny's for a Moons Over My Hammy). The Psycho is an equal-opportunity liar, spinning tales about everything from how she met her latest boyfriend (you have a feeling that "in line at Crate and Barrel" really means "online in the Casual Encounters section of Craigslist") to her financial situation. (It's slightly suspect that a freelance assistant events planner could afford a Marc Jacobs bag.) You've got to hand it to her, though: the Psycho is such a convincing liar that she would make a great publicist.

2. Disappearing Acts: The last time you checked, a mani-pedi takes an hour, maybe two if you spring for the extra foot massage. Yet when the Psycho says she'll call you when she gets back from the nail salon, it could be hours, days, and or even weeks before you hear from her again. You would issue an Amber Alert if this was one of your saner friends, but the psycho loves to pull the Houdini act. It doesn't matter where she went—she could be skiing in Jackson Hole or lost in a K-hole for all you know—because one thing is certain: like a cold sore, she always manages to pop back into you life at the worst possible time.

3. Shiny Penny Syndrome: Tree hugger, emo chick, party girl, punk princess. No, this isn't the casting call for another teen movie. These are the different personas the Psycho has tried on in the last ten minutes. Whether she's running off to an ashram in the mountains for an intensive yoga workshop or potty training her new puggle, the Psycho quickly becomes obsessed with something new, loses interest, and moves on, just like K-Fed with his first two kids.

4. Powerfully Persuasive: The Psycho has this ability to get you to do things that you wouldn't normally do. In your younger years, you had a blast as she pushed you out of your comfort zone. (She convinced you to go bungee jumping, try out for the volleyball team, and make a move on that hot Jeremy/Jason London look-alike who worked behind the counter at the record store.) Lately, though, it seems like the Psycho is making you an unwilling accomplice to her craziness, like that one time she picked you up at your place to go to a 7:15 movie but first had to run a couple of errands (and by "run a couple of errands" we mean that she tossed a brick through the front window of her ex's new girlfriend's house while you sat in the passenger seat of her car and obliviously scanned the radio for good songs).

Psycho Babelfish: Your Crazy Talk Translator

While she may tell it like it is when it comes to other people's business, the Psycho is less forthcoming about herself. Here, we translate her crazy talk.

What She Says	What It Really Means
We've stopped seeing each other.	The restraining order prevents me from being within three hundred yards of him.
I got it on sale.	I snuck it into my purse while the store security guard was bending over and tying his shoe.
I've become very spiritual lately.	I'm banging my yoga instructor.
I've been promoted to supervisor at work.	Managing the voices in my head is a full-time job.
I need to work out some stuff on my own right now.	They tried to make me go to rehab, I said no, no, no.
I think I'm staying in tonight.	My drug dealer delivers.
I guess I'm just a very sexual person.	I have more issues than *National Geographic*.
I'm close to my family.	I once made out with my second cousin.
Dontcha wish your girlfriend was hot like me?	Mine isn't an exit only.
I'm really a nice girl . . . until you cross me.	It puts the lotion in the basket.

Why You Love the Psycho: Much like Camel Reds or your great-aunt Nettie, the Psycho doesn't have much of an internal filter and therefore says the things you only wish you could.

Example: After checking out an annoying coworker's engagement ring, she said, "You must give really good head."

Why She Sometimes Irks You: Considering she has been (self-) diagnosed with a litany of disorders, dysfunctions, phobias, and philias, she has little interest in anyone else's issues.

Example: When you told the Psycho that you broke up with your boyfriend of three years, she started sobbing uncontrollably about the boy who dumped her three years ago.

How to Be a Better Friend to the Psycho: As long as you keep being an enabler, then nobody is gonna get hurt.

How Your Friendship Will Fare: No so good, but she'll probably befriend the voices in her head and forget all about you.

Where she'll be in ten years: In group therapy at Promises with Maddox Jolie-Pitt and the *Little Miss Sunshine* girl (you know she's an *E! True Hollywood Story* waiting to happen).

Basket-Case Robin: 31 Flavors of Psycho

Not all Psycho friends are created the same. Here is a sampling of the various kinds of crazy that they come in.

- **The Worker Bee-yotch Psycho:** She suffers from a debilitating condition that gives her sociopathic tendencies in the workplace yet still allows her to act relatively functional and human outside of the office. When she and her husband chat you up while wearing big smiles and matching polo shirts at the annual company picnic, you almost feel bad about that one time you photocopied your ass on the color Xerox and blamed it on her. Almost.

- **The Size 00 Psycho:** Everything about her is normal except that she hasn't eaten since 1997.
- **The Single White Female Psycho:** Your friendship with her starts off pretty normal, but it quickly deteriorates when she becomes overly possessive and jealous. She's basically your ex-boyfriend, only with less back hair.
- **The Happy Hour Psycho:** By day, she's a PowerPointing, Excel spreadsheeting mastermind, but once she clocks out and downs a few sea breezes at the local post-work spot, she'll inevitably end up flashing someone and drunk dialing her married boss from behind the Big Game Hunter machine.
- **The Boy Crazy Psycho:** When you decided to shun the traditional Spring Break booze-and-boy fest in favor of an all-girl's spa trip, she refused to speak to you for months.
- **The Psycho-in-Remission:** She appears to have grown out of dancing on tables, pulling hair in girl fights, and getting tattoos in Sanskrit. However, deep down you know that she's a breakup away from tossing out the pearls and bringing back the vials of blood.
- **The Aspiring Actress Psycho:** The Aspiring Actress Psycho loves being the loudest person in the room, having romantic intrigue with her fellow T.G.I. Friday's employees, and making out with her gay guy friends "just for fun." Interestingly enough, her level of psychosis diminishes once her parents stop paying her rent.
- **The Postal Psycho:** She's the real deal: neither snow nor rain nor heat nor gloom of night keeps her from delivering the crazy.

Sounding Off:
Livin' La Vida Loca

Below, real women talk about the highs and lows of the most chemically unbalanced friend in their social circle (or, as we lovingly call her, the Psycho). Seriously, we couldn't make up this kind of craziness if we tried.

"My psycho friend is an acquired taste. She's loyal, but incredibly territorial about her boyfriend. I love her to death, but really, did she need to run his stereo speakers over with her car when they were in a fight? And as funny as it was at the time, I'm not positive she absolutely had to throw a table at our other friend at a very crowded party when she saw her engaged in conversation with the aforementioned boyfriend. Never a dull moment with that one." —Molly, 22

"My psycho friend is as upfront with her psychoness as, well, a complete psycho. She will attack anyone in her path, bombarding them with questions while simultaneously releasing a deluge of her issues onto the scene. She is manic to the point of acting like a child that just escaped from Willy Wonka's chocolate factory and then turns off like a switch into her reserved, quiet, and incredibly morose counterpart. People can spot her crazy from a mile away, which is fine by her because she claims that she has nothing to hide." —Mary, 28

"When my psycho friend found out that her boyfriend was cheating on her, she set a bunch of stuff he gave her on fire in the middle of the street." —Lauren, 21

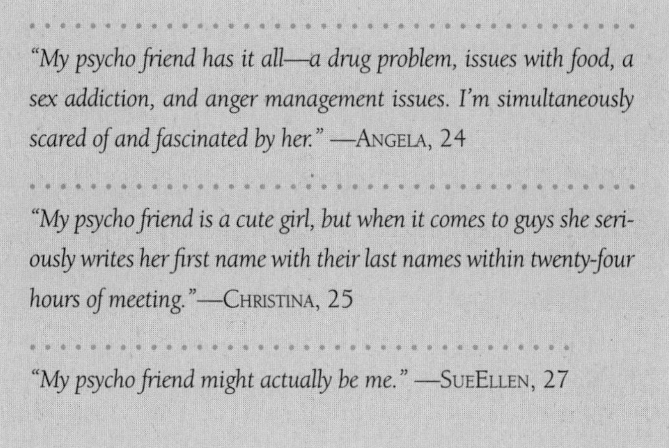

"My psycho friend has it all—a drug problem, issues with food, a sex addiction, and anger management issues. I'm simultaneously scared of and fascinated by her." —Angela, 24

"My psycho friend is a cute girl, but when it comes to guys she seriously writes her first name with their last names within twenty-four hours of meeting."—Christina, 25

"My psycho friend might actually be me." —SueEllen, 27

Should You Stay or Should You Go?: Determining If This "Friendship" Is Worth Saving

"Mean people suck" read the bumper sticker that every neo-hippy with a trust fund slapped on her Volvo or Jetta back in high school. We couldn't agree more. Mean people suck, and life is too short to spend torturing yourself with sucky mean people who masquerade as your friends. As we've established in this chapter, when it comes to frenemies, *mean* comes in many forms, from the blatant nastiness of unfriendly competition and backstabbing to the passive aggressiveness of jealousy and enabling. And, pardon us for a Dr. Phil interlude, but one stereotype about women really is true: we have this tendency to hang on to relationships that are well past their expiration dates because we don't want to hurt anyone's feelings—except our own. If you're wondering whether it's time to cut off ties with a frenemy, ask yourself: Is this sort of friendship actually worth it?

If you still have your doubts, take a deeper look at your so-called friendship. Has interacting with your frenemy caused you to experience any of the following symptoms? And be honest with yourself, because the first step to recovery is admitting that you have a problem.

- Headache
- Fever
- Chills
- Decreased appetite
- Exhaustion
- Nausea
- Diarrhea

If you answered yes to any of the above, you may have influenza, which is bad. Go see a doctor. On the other hand, if you even had to consult this list, it's probably time to remove your frenemy from your buddy list. Remember: the only physical ailment a good friend is supposed to give you is the occasional hangover. Okay. If you're still not sure if she's a friend or a frenemy, check out the following quiz. (And for tips on bidding her adieu, see Chapter Twelve: "When the Friendship Sinks: Breaking Up, Making Up, and Moving On." However, if you're trying to break free from the Psycho or the Ike Turner, you might be better off getting a restraining order.)

Pop Quiz: Is She a Friend or a Frenemy?

Like John Travolta's hair, some friends seem genuine at first, but upon closer inspection, they turn out to be high-quality fakes. If you're still questioning a certain friend's authenticity, sharpen your no. 2 pencil because it's time for a pop quiz. There're no wrong answers here, but be forewarned: It might be unpleasant to find out that your "friend" doesn't have your back so much as she's likely to stab you in it.

1. **Your friend gives you a present for your birthday. What's your initial reaction?**
   a. You're pleasantly surprised by her thoughtfulness. After all, you can never have too many pairs of edible underwear.
   b. You feel a little guilty since you didn't get her a gift for her birthday. Come to think of it, you forgot her birthday entirely.
   c. You're suspicious of her motives, so you call up Homeland Security and have them send a bomb-sniffing dog and one of those robotic arms to investigate the package.
2. **Which relationship between two characters on *The Hills* most closely resembles your friendship?**
   a. Lauren and Audrina: She comforts you when Brody hooks up with a random ho and you tell her that Justin Bobby is a total toolbox.
   b. Lauren and Whitney: She listens to you whine every day about your never-ending made-for-TV drama and you invite her to lunch when Audrina is too busy riding around on the back of Justin Bobby's motorcycle.
   c. Lauren and Heidi: She thinks you're controlling and manipula-

tive. You think some of the silicone has leaked to her brain, causing irreparable damage.

3. **You and your friend are in charge of throwing a bridal shower. Which song best describes your collaborative efforts:**
   a. "It Takes Two" by Rob Base and DJ E-Z Rock
   b. "Bossy" by Kelis
   c. "I'm a Slave 4 U" by Britney Spears
4. **You invite your friends over to your place for a potluck dinner party. She offers to bring:**
   a. An appetizer and a six pack of beer
   b. An appetizer, a main course, a dessert, and a case of wine
   c. Nothing. Hell, who knows if she'll even show up.
5. **Complete the following sentence. Your boyfriend thinks that she is . . .**
   a. so cool that he offered to set her up with one of his friends.
   b. a little creepy. Why does she have a lock of your hair in her wallet?
   c. scarier than Pinhead from *Hellraiser.*
6. **Complete the following analogy: She : me ::**
   a. Beavis : Butt-Head
   b. Marcie : Peppermint Patty
   c. Mr. Burns : Smithers
7. **You splurged on a fancy-schmancy designer purse. Her reaction is:**
   a. She oohs and aahs and makes you promise to let her borrow it.
   b. She buys you special leather cleaner and offers to buff out any scratches you get on it.
   c. She asks if it's a knockoff or asks you if you are aware of how many alligators, baby cows, or pieces of canvas had to suffer for your vanity and consumerism.

8. **You and your friend run into your ex and he's with his new girlfriend. Afterward she says:**
   a. "You're way prettier than she is."
   b. Nothing. She's too busy tackling the girl and spraying Mace in her eyes.
   c. "Wow, do you think she's a model?"
9. **While out to lunch together, you tell your friend about the big promotion you just got at work. She:**
   a. Orders a celebratory round of drinks.
   b. Picks up the tab, then treats you to a pedicure.
   c. Yawns, then starts talking about how her company is sending her to their Paris office in the spring.
10. **You're most likely to call her when . . .**
   a. You need someone who will listen.
   b. You're feeling down and need an ego boost.
   c. You're bored and no one else is picking up their phone.

If you answered . . .

Mostly A's: You've Got a Friend

She sounds more supportive than a sports bra, which is exactly the way a friend should be. Congratulations—you can pass Go and collect $200.

Mostly B's: You've Got a Mini Me

Although it might not seem like it, there's definitely a frenemy in this friendship—she just happens to be you. Whether she volunteered to be your minion or you somehow manipulated her into accepting the position, it's time to set your indentured servant free and learn how to treat other people better. In fact, read this book again. And again. Come to think of it, buy a new copy every time you reread it. That'll teach you.

Mostly C's: You've Got a Frenemy

It's true that some relationships have a love-hate/sibling rivalry aspect to them, but if your "friend" falls in this category, then she's actually a frenemy. So, unless you like to hurt so good (and if you do, check out the appropriately named "Hurt So Good: Constructive Masochistic Activities," for some painful alternatives to being involved in a toxic friendship), stop wasting your time, ditch the bitch, and find something else to complain about. Now, make a positive change in your life and imagine yourself soldiering on, frenemy-free, with an enpowering KT Tunstall song playing in the background.

Hurt So Good: Constructive Masochistic Activities

If you're going to keep sticking your hand in the fire and getting burned, why not actually get something out of it? Here are ten frenemy-free constructive ways to inflict pain on yourself.

- Get a tattoo (but not a navel piercing—way too Spring Break 1999. Actually, don't get a dolphin tattoo, either, which is Spring Break 1994).
- Eat some habanera peppers (spicy food is good for you).
- Have the hair on your bikini line lasered off.
- Try that freaky bendy yoga shit that keeps Madonna in Bionic Woman shape.
- Take snowboarding lessons (instead of breaking your heart you'll break your ass).

- Get a root canal without Novocain. (Paging James Frey.)
- Read *Finnegans Wake*.
- Two words: *colon cleanse*.
- Organize that miscellaneous junk drawer (or drawers) in your kitchen/bedroom/office.
- Take a defensive driving class.

Ms. Friendship Manners

Dear Ms. Friendship Manners,

A close friend of mine got herself into a bit of trouble, and by trouble, I mean that she racked up a $20,000 MasterCard bill. Now, she's struggling to make her minimum payments and pay her rent. She asked me if she could borrow some money to help get her through the rest of the month. I don't know what to do. I want to help out a friend in need, but I doubt that she'll ever pay me back.

Sincerely confused,
Not a trust-fund baby in Toledo

Dear Not a Trust-Fund Baby,

As Ms. Friendship Manners has stressed time and time again, money will always come between friends. Also, how exactly did your friend incur so much debt? Does she have a gambling problem or is she addicted to home shopping? Some time after the demise of Ms. Friendship Manners's first marriage, she had a very impolite evening with a bottle of brandy and ended up buying a Soloflex Bow machine from an infomercial.

Here is the general rule for lending money to your friends: Don't lend money to your friends. If you want to help someone out monetarily, give cash as a gift and don't expect to be paid back. Of course, there are exceptions to the money-lending rule. Feel free to loan a friend some dough if she needs bus fare or if her life is in jeopardy and you are the only one who can save her. Just keep this in mind: no matter how convincing her argument, she won't actually die if she doesn't buy that new Gucci bag.

Sounding Off: True Crimes in Friendship History

Sometimes a so-called friend commits an offense so heinous (and sadly, it often involves a guy), it makes you wonder why you ever liked her in the first place. When reading these "oh no she didn't" tales of dishonesty, manipulation, and bitchery, notice the repeated use of "best friends," in quotes. If this doesn't inspire you to cut a frenemy loose or at least be thankful for the great people in your life, we don't know what will.

"In college, my roommate slept with my boyfriend while I was home for Thanksgiving and they stayed at school. I didn't find out until about a month later, when her sorority sisters ratted her out. Worst part, she wasn't even that cute." —MEREDITH, 24

"My friend pulled my boyfriend into a bathroom and told him that she couldn't orgasm and that I had told her he was really good in bed and said that they should have sex—right now! He told her that he would like to have a drink first, gave her $5, grabbed me, and left the bar. Outside he yelled at me asking why I would 'rent him out to my best friend.' She of course, denied the whole thing." —KELLY, 25

"When my friend's parents asked her why money was missing from her trust fund, she told them that I stole it. In reality, she took her own money for drugs. Needless to say, we are no longer friends." —STACEY, 30

"After spending months talking to my 'best friend 'and roommate about how I had a huge crush on this guy whom I'd been flirting and spending a lot of time with, she got wasted one night, struck up a conversation with him about how they both knew me, and hooked up with him in our room, while I was 'sleeping.' In the morning she lied about it, but after about a week, she finally admitted to what had happened." —MOLLY, 22

"My 'best friend' in college broke the cardinal rule of not dating a guy that I had been involved with for about a year and a half. I caught them in the bathroom of our dorm. I then found out that they had been dating for six months. I haven't spoken to either of

them since. Oh, and they only lasted about another month after they came clean."—Alison, 25

"My friend stole my car when she was wasted and totaled it. And it's not like the keys were lying around—she took my whole bag with her." —Samantha, 27

chapter seven

LIKE KISSING YOUR BROTHER

Boy Friends

Although this book is mostly about you and your girls, we couldn't help but spend a little time on the guys in our lives. It's a classic love story, only with a platonic twist: Girl meets boy and sparks fly as they discuss the things in life that *really* matter, like which was better, Van Halen with Diamond Dave or Sammy Hagar, or whatever happened to the McRib? That shit was tasty. And, for a host of reasons, ranging from timing (you're already in a romantic relationship with a great guy) to attraction (you like boys and so does he), the two of you are better off as friends.

We live in a society that salivates over the ooey-gooey popcorn flick notion that coed friendships are only a means to end, which usually takes place in the form of a Hollywood ending: either the woman runs barefoot through the rain to stop her best buddy at the altar from marrying the wrong woman (that is, someone who isn't her) or the man runs through a crowded airport to proclaim his love to his friend before she boards a flight to Africa and disappears from his life forever. (After all, why should she leave and try to help some strangers eat when she can stay home and shop for new salad bowls with him at Pottery Barn?)

Now, before you start thinking that we're totally unromantic and stuff, hear us out: Sure, many a love affair has blossomed from a strong, platonic friendship, and friendship is an important component in every love affair. One of the greatest poets of our time, Michael Bolton, summed it up best: "How can we be lovers if we can't be friends?" We wholeheartedly agree, but we'd also like to add a line: "How can we be friends only with people who have a vajayjay?"

Ask a hundred different people for their takes on coed friendship and you're bound to tune out after five minutes and start thinking about more pressing matters, like who's going to get eliminated from *Top Chef* tonight. There are many schools of thought regarding male-female nonsexual relations, ranging from pre-K (gender is a nonissue when it comes to the people you buddy up to; it's all about who has the best toys) to adult education (men and women can't be friends because sex is always going to get in the way). We tend to think along the lines of a $25,000 per year touchy-feely private school where the students get "evaluations" rather than grades and are encouraged to follow their "inner spirit": the success of boy-girl friendships really depends on the individual. However, if you can get past preconceived notions of how men and women are supposed to interact with each other, you'll make it to the honor roll and benefit from some great new friendships.

Girlfriends are a given, boyfriends come and go, and here are a few good reasons to incorporate some testosterone into your knitting circle:

Better Living Without Chemistry: Why You Need Guy Friends

- Because your air conditioner isn't going to install itself.
- Because it's good to get a male perspective from sources other than *Maxim* and *Entourage.*
- Because every once in a while it's nice to spend time with a person who doesn't have the same cycle as you.
- Because someone besides your cat needs to appreciate your burping skills.
- Because if you have to spend money on an engagement party, bridal shower, bridesmaid dress, bachelorette party, and wedding gift, you'd like to bring along a guest who will actually join you on the dance floor as you do the Macarena.
- Because you need someone to explain *Donnie Darko* and *Mulholland Dr.* to you.
- Because your real brother lives three thousand miles away.
- Because some bugs really are the size of small dogs.
- Because sometimes it's nice to be with someone who still thinks South Beach is a place, not a diet.

Typecasting: Your History with Men

Boy friends come in all shapes, sizes, and sexual orientations. Here are the most likely types to cross your path. You'll notice that many of these male friend archetypes involve some sort of romantic innuendos, which is kind of inevitable as long as moms continue to be nosy and Hollywood keeps cranking out date movies centered around friends falling in love.

- **The Kevin Arnold, a.k.a., Your Brother from Another Mother (and if you want to get technical, he's from another father, too, but that doesn't rhyme):** You two go waaay back to a time when he used Stridex pads and wore "husky" sizes and you had braces and booblets. He's so much like real family that even slow dancing with him seems a bit incestuous. Your close-knit relationship doesn't prevent your mother from getting in her little comments about you and the Kevin Arnold someday tying the knot and making mini Winnie Coopers.

  How to Deal: Hell's not freezing over (thanks to global warming), the fat lady has laryngitis, and you and the Kevin Arnold will never live happily ever after—at least, not with each other. The next time you're at a family function and a relative makes one of those annoying remarks about how you and your surrogate brother would make such a cute couple, lean in really close and whisper, "We tried a couple of times, but he couldn't get it up." Make hand gestures to really get your point across.

- **The Pit Bull:** The Pit Bull is a real dog. He treats his girlfriends (an endless parade of big breasted, small-brained blondes with lower self-worth than wet T-shirt contest contestants) like crap and talks down to waitstaff. While you'd never want to date him or serve him dinner, he's surprisingly warm and protective as a friend, or, at least, he's warm and protective compared to how he treats others in his life. You just thank your lucky stars that you're on his good side.

  How to Deal: A word of caution: no matter how many times he asks you to set him up with one of your friends ("a hot one—not one who has a 'good personality'"), resist the urge. Also, keep some pepper spray on hand because the Pit Bull may be friendly for the time being, but due to the unpredictable nature of his breed, he will bite when you least expect it. Plus, do you really want to be friends with someone who pays for only one newspaper, but actually takes four out of the vending machine?

- **The Possibility:** He's good enough, he's smart enough, and, gosh darnit, why don't you like him? The Possibility is a great catch—cute, funny, successful, and a perfect boy friend—yet he's lacking that intangible something that would make him the perfect *boyfriend*. You chalk it up to chemistry, since one woman's Mark Wahlberg is another woman's Donnie, and vice versa. (To be fair, he probably feels the same way about you.) However, the lack of a spark doesn't stop you from wondering during your more vulnerable moments about the possibility of the Possibility fitting into your life in a not-so-platonic way.

  How to Deal: The next time you have a few cocktails and start to think of the Possibility in a biblical sense, take a nice, long *Crying Game* shower.

- **The Action Figure:** The Action Figure prefers a little less conversation, a little more action. If you want to spend hours eating ice cream and talking about your hopes, dreams, and fears, look elsewhere. (See page 127, "The Gal Pal—Your Number-One Gay.") Your relationship with the Action Figure thrives on constant motion: He's your gym buddy, tennis partner, hiking companion, and Ultimate Frisbee teammate. He'll always be up for seeing the latest movie, visiting the hottest new club, and checking out the next big thing (*They sound kinda like Daft Punk meets*

Nick Drake meets Willie Nelson) in a dark little downtown hole-in-the-wall on a Wednesday night.

How to Deal: Save your ruminations for a friend who loves touchy-feely, self-help talk (once again, page 127, "The Gal Pal—Your Number-One Gay") and just sit back and enjoy the adrenaline boost you get from your Action Figure.

✦ **The Ex-Boyfriend:** Usually, "let's just be friends" means something along the lines of, "Sure, let's get together sometime. How about never? Does never work for you?" But, much to the shock of your girls and the dismay of your significant other, you've managed to stay friendly with a guy who has seen you in many a compromising position. Maintaining a friendship with an ex is possible if both parties involved act like mature adults and stay within the boundaries of appropriateness. Yeah . . . and John Travolta really is straight as an arrow.

How to Deal: Your level of friend success with the Ex-Boyfriend depends on several factors: 1. The seriousness of your relationship when you were dating. (Were you together for three weeks in college or did you waste the best years of your life with him or, at least, the years when your hair looked the best?) 2. The amount of time that has passed since you broke up and the severity of the split. (Did you end the affair by passing him a note in homeroom or did he tell you last week that he no longer loved you and gave you two days to find a new apartment?) 3. The amount of evidence that you have moved on. (Are you both involved with other people or do you have to resist the urge to spin your head around *Exorcist*-style and barf up pea soup every time you see him talking to a woman who isn't his mother or his sister?). Evaluate all of these factors and act accordingly. If you still carry a torch for the Ex-Boyfriend, it's probably for the best to deprive it of oxygen.

- **The Friend with Benefits:** You're full-time friends and part-time lovers. But, if it's such a win-win situation, why do you sometimes feel like you're cheating yourself? Maybe it's because he's never asked you on an actual date, you've never hung out together during the day (leaving his place after the sun comes up doesn't count), and you're not entirely sure what his occupation is (lawyer? banker? Chippendales dancer?). And while you don't find him particularly attractive, smart, or funny, none of that matters after you've had a few mojitos (sobriety eludes you in this friendship), your prospects at the bar are limited to a guy with a lazy eye, and your Friend with Benefits is just a booty-text away.

  How to Deal: If the only benefit you're getting from this friend is a warm body in your bed and that uh-oh feeling in the morning, it might be time to delete his number from your phone, or, better yet, set him up with an acquaintance who might actually learn his last name.

- **The Flirt:** There's just something about this guy that makes you want to twirl your hair around your finger and bat your eyelashes. Your friendship is based on anticipation and sexual innuendos (is that an iPod in his pocket or is he just happy to see you?) and you can always count on the Flirt to whisper something dirty in your ear, wink at you from across the room, or grab your ass when you walk by. Yet, despite numerous opportunities to make good on all of your naughty promises, you haven't so much as kissed, which is ironic considering everyone thinks that you've been banging for years.

How to Deal: Once he gets a girlfriend and tries to talk to you without making suggestive comments, the conversation has less substance than one of the Olsen twins' straight-to-DVD movies.

- **The Self-Proclaimed Guy's Girl (aka, the Self-Hating Guy's Girl):** So we're cheating a little by sneaking a girl in here, but we promise that it makes total sense. Even though she doesn't have the proper guy equipment (that is, chromosomes, a penis, and whatnot), the Self-Proclaimed Guy's Girl considers herself "just one of the guys." Don't confuse her with the tomboy next door or that chick in that eighties movie who pretends to be a dude, since the only balls the guy's girl wants to play with are the kind that don't bounce. She claims that she doesn't hang out with other chicks because they're too much drama and have jealousy issues. This is usually a roundabout way of saying, "I need attention" or "I have Shannen Doherty tendencies."

  How to Deal: Even though her shtick is more transparent to you than a freshly Windexed windshield, it's not worth trying to explain it to your guy friends since they'll just make hissing cat noises and suggest that you mud wrestle with her.
- **The Crush:** Whenever he walks into a room (in slow motion, of course, with "Wicked Games" playing in the background) you turn an alarming shade of crimson. You secretly want to bang him—or, at least, you think it's secret. If you still had a Trapper Keeper, you'd write your initials with a heart around them and practice signing your would-be married name. He's your Jake Ryan, your Tad

Hamilton, or your Troy Bolton (that's Zac Efron, for those of you born before 1990). Of course, he's dating the head cheerleader—a total bimbo who likes him only because he drives a convertible, and who doesn't appreciate that he is a sensitive individual who writes poetry and wants to go to art school, not Princeton like his father. (Okay, so none of that last part is true but just go with it.) So unless your life magically turns into a romantic comedy in which the Crush will fall in love with you in the next 90 minutes, you'll have to drool over him (and his perfect ass) from afar.

How to Deal: If you haven't already memorized his schedule, taken up the same hobbies as him, and plucked a hair from his head (for a love spell, obviously) then do so immediately. Once you've completed phase one, you can move on to phase two, in which you start dating his best friend in an attempt to make your crush jealous. Hey, it worked for us in middle school. That, and stuffing our bras with our moms' shoulder pads.

- **The Duckie:** For years your girlfriends have been teasing you about having your own stalker, but you remain oblivious to the Duckie's love, and insist that he is just a good friend who really likes doing nice things for you. After all, didn't he beg you to let him detail your car? So in a way it's like you were doing him a favor, right? Just keep telling yourself that. Every now and again the Duckie will grow tired of being on the crap end of the unrequited love stick and attempt to distance himself from you. But inevitably he'll give up on giving up and resume his role as the guy you love like a brother.

  How to Deal: Resist the urge to use the Duckie just to

boost your ego, since we all know how tough it can be to have a crush on someone who thinks that you are "sweet" (if not, reread "The Crush" above). If it's unconditional love and unlimited affection you need, adopt a pug or a kid or something.

- **The Person:** Men are from Mars, women are from Venus, and it's hopeless to think we'll ever be able to get along, right? So imagine your surprise when you strike up a friendship with a guy not because he's a possible romantic interest or because he knows his way around a toolbox, but simply because you like him for the Person that he is. In fact, you're so blind to the Person's gender that he's kind of like Pat from *Saturday Night Live*. And because his maleness doesn't get in the way of things, your relationship with him is one of the most functional you've ever had.

  How to Deal: Um, just continue having fun, you know, person to the Person.

Friend in Focus: The Gal Pal—Your Gay Best Friend

What's His Deal?: When you were a little girl, you dreamed of having your very own fairy godmother, a regal woman, who, with a wave of her magic wand, could transform you from an awkward little girl with scabby knees and frizzy curls to a pretty, pretty princess. In reality, what you got was something that can't be found in a Disney movie (although we've always had our suspicions about Sebastian from *The Little Mermaid*). The Gal Pal is your gay best friend, your right-hand man, and your soul mate minus the sex. With a wave of his highlighting wand, he can transform you from mousy brunette to honey-hued blonde, and, unlike the curfew-enforcing grandma in *Cinderella*, your Gal Pal would never make you go home at midnight on a Friday because that's when the Blue Collar Boys Bash at the Man Hole starts to pick up.

To be fair, not all hetero men are the beer, broads, and boobs types and not all gay men just stepped off the set of *Queer Eye for the Straight Guy*. (See page 131, "Shades of Gay," for a look at all types of gay besties.) However, even if your Gal Pal didn't shed a tear when you bought your first pair of Jimmy Choos and hasn't been wearing a full face of makeup since his bar mitzvah, his interests are probably more sophisticated than those of your other (straight-as-an-arrow) guy friends. For starters, while they're into Dan Patrick on ESPN and keep fit on the basketball court, your Gal Pal gets his news fix via a Prada-clad Anderson Cooper and prefers to break a sweat in the sauna at the gym.

And, while it may seem like Gal Pals have become as tired as competitive reality shows, there's a legitimate reason why all of your friends want well-groomed boys who like boys to accessorize their arms like wait-listed "It" bags: a Gal Pal will offer you a muscular shoulder to lean on and a well-manicured hand to hold without ever expecting something more titillating out of the exchange.

How You Met: He sat next to your mother at Celine Dion's "A New Day" concert in Vegas. Your mom thought he was "charming" and tried to set you up with him. To this day, she insists that your Gal Pal seemed totally straight, despite the fact that he cried during "My Heart Will Go On."

Symptoms of the Gal Pal:

1. Sexless Soulmates: When you're not working or hanging out with your girlfriends, you and your Gal Pal take wine-tasting classes, go salsa dancing, and have weekend sleepovers. He also takes you to candlelit dinners at five-star restaurants, calls you at bedtime to say good night, and buys you fancy lingerie for your birthday. You would love to have a boyfriend do all those things for you, but you're *way* too busy to date. Plus, chances are that he'll never smell as good as your gay bestie.

2. Honesty Is His Only Policy: When you tried on a pair of "lay down on the bed to zip them up" skinny jeans for one of your female friends, she swore on her life that you looked "totally hot" in them. Your Gal Pal let you know the truth. The moment you limped through the front door of his apartment wearing the skin-tight denim he said, "You look like a Jenny Craig 'before' photo." (*That was way harsh, Tai.*) Just because your Gal Pal appears to be more sensitive than the average straight male doesn't mean he actually is. On the flip side, when he gives you a compliment, you know he's being honest. (When he told you that your "lovely lady lumps" looked hot in that tank top, you swelled with pride.)

3. Unlucky in Love: The Gal Pal is your only other friend who is more screwed up about men than you are. The two of you spend hours comparing notes from your respective therapy sessions, swap self-help books (he recommended *Women Who Love Too Much*), and trade clichés like "there are no good men left" and "guys are such assholes these days" over boozy brunches.

4. Noncompete Clause: Unfortunately, there sometimes can be a feeling of competition between girlfriends. If your GBF had XY chromosomes, you'd feel tinges of jealousy. He has flawless skin, abs of steel, a year-round tan, and a closet full of designer denim, plush cashmere, and overpriced shoes. Okay, perhaps you still get a little disappointed when you realize that the hot guy checking you out is actually cruising your Gal Pal.

Your Best Girlfriend Versus the Gal Pal

One holds your hair back when you've had too much to drink and the other tells you when your hair looks like vomit. They may not always see eye to eye (your best girl friend wasn't thrilled when your gal pal offered to give her a makeover) but they do share a passion for boys, bronzer, and being your friend. Here's a closer look at the mismatched bookends that support you no matter what.

	Your Best Girlfriend	Your Gal Pal
Skincare regime	Clinique 3-Step	In a twelve-step program for La Mer addiction
Madonna karaoke song	"Like a Virgin"	"Material Girl"
Favorite drama	*Grey's Anatomy*	*Grey Gardens*
Her/His idea of a great night out	Good wine, good conversation, and hot boy eye candy	Good wine, good conversation, and hot boy eye candy
Beloved pet	Murray, a Lab-something mix she rescued from the pound	Guster, an Italian greyhound who used to show at Westminster
Your biggest fight	You borrowed her favorite push-up bra for a wedding and left it in the best man's hotel room	He borrowed your favorite push-up bra for "Icon Night" at the gay bar and accidentally left it in "Guyza Minelli's" apartment after he spent the night there
Preferred footwear	Whatever is comfortable and on sale at Nine West	Whatever is overpriced and brand-new at the Prada store
Strength	A great listener	A great listener—and dresser
Weakness	Emotionally unavailable men and Twizzlers	Emotionally unavailable men and Baked Lays
Best Halloween Costume	J.Lo circa her P. Diddy days	J.Lo circa her "Jenny from the Block" days
Dirty Secret	Once made out with a girl during Spring Break	Once made out with a girl during Spring Break

Why You Love the Gal Pal: He makes every event bigger, better, and more exciting.

Example: He hosts catered viewing parties at his apartment for everything from *Project Runway* and *Top Chef* to the Westminster Dog Show and the Miss America pageant.

Why He Sometimes Irks You: He can be picky, overcritical, and judgmental.

Example: You rejected a perfectly nice (and straight!) guy after your GBF pointed out that he had a slight lisp.

How to Be a Better Friend to the Gal Pal: Even if his relationship drama involves a love triangle between a ballet dancer and a closeted soap opera actor, try to take his romantic encounters seriously. It may seem like his love life exists purely for your entertainment, but he'll probably find his Prince Charming before you do. Oh snap.

How Your Friendship Will Fare: After a mutual two-year "breakup," you got back together when he asked you to be the "best woman" in his upcoming nuptials to Randy, an antiques dealer he met at the White Party in Palm Springs. Knowing that he'd pick out something amazing for you to wear, you happily obliged and lived happily ever after as gay man and best girl friend.

Where the Gal Pal Will Be in Ten Years: Hosting a lavish, catered party (complete with Kobe beef sliders and grilled mahi-mahi) to celebrate the second birthday of Harold, the boy he and Randy adopted from Malawi. You'll be there, of course.

Shades of Gay: Celebrating the Diversity of Gay Best Friends

Despite what you see on television—specifically reality shows about makeovers, competitive dancing, and interior decorating—

all gays aren't created equal. That said, there's nothing wrong with a little categorizing between friends, right?

- **The 4 Percent Body Fat Gay:** He's super-masculine, obsessed with the gym, and drinks, rather than eats, eggs. To him, a gay man without a gym membership is like a straight woman who doesn't love jewelry—unnatural and just plain wrong.

  Think: He-Man (It all makes sense: the shiny blond bob, the metallic miniskirt, and you know that She-Ra was his beard.)
- **The Metro/Ambiguous Gay:** While it isn't known for sure if he's gay (he never gives you a straight answer when you ask him, pun totally intended), all the signs seem to suggest that he plays for the pink team; lots of product in his hair, jeans that are just a bit too tight, and a subscription to *Details*.

  Think: Ryan Seacrest
- **The Fashionista:** His favorite adjectives are *genius* and *fierce,* he prefers French *Vogue* to the American version, and counts Joan Crawford and Nanook of the North as his muses. You wouldn't dare wear synthetic fabrics in his presence, lest he get all Karl Lagerfeld on your poly-blend ass.

  Think: Michael Kors and Isaac Mizrahi
- **The All Hail to the Queen:** He calls himself a "divo," wears bedazzled velour tracksuits, and is prone to temper tantrums. When he's not ruling his imaginary kingdom, he works in sales, lives with his mother, and polishes his "crown" (which is really a rhinestone tiara from Claire's Accessories).

  Think: Damian from *Mean Girls*

- **The Drama Club Gay:** His childhood dream was to be on *The All New Mickey Mouse Club* with Justin, Britney, and Christina but his mother wouldn't let him audition (he's still working out his anger issues in therapy). He's seen *Rent* thirty-two times, has played Danny in *Grease* on seven different occasions, and will totally get it on with a girl (if the script calls for it, that is).

  Think: Lance Bass
- **The White-Collar Gay:** He's an Ivy League–educated professional with a closetful of custom-made monogrammed shirts and a corner office. When he's not working a sixty-hour week, he likes to drink espresso and read *The Wall Street Journal* on the deck of his beach house in the Hamptons.

  Think: Will Truman
- **The Power Gay:** He runs the show and calls the shots—usually from the comfort of his Gulfstream G500 (the seats are monogrammed with his initials, natch). And when his custom-made Italian leather loafers are on the ground, he hobnobs with the rich and famous at various awards shows, fund-raisers, and any other event that has passed hors d'ouvres and an ice sculpture.

  Think: David Geffen
- **The Who Woulda Thunk Gay:** Once it came out that Ashlee Simpson doesn't actually sing, few things in life really shock you. But you were truly stunned when you found out that this particular guy was gay. He doesn't own a single Madonna CD, he doesn't like musicals, and he played football in high school.

  Think: Tinky Winky and SpongeBob SquarePants
- **The Mentor:** Nurturing, level-headed, and honest, he's the

gay you go to when you have a problem and need some no-nonsense advice but don't want to ask your father. And because he wears glasses, has gray hair, and listens only to classical music, by default he's the smartest person you know.

Think: Tim Gunn

- **The Why Oh Why Does He Have to Be Gay Gay:** He's gorgeous, funny, sweet, and smart. He'd be the perfect boyfriend—except he likes boys.

  Think: Danny from *The Real World: New Orleans*

Ten Things to Hate About Me: Use These Clues from Teen Movies to Let a Guy Know that You Just Want to Be Friends

No matter how many times a particular male friend has said to you, "You're like a sister to me," a part of him can't help picturing you naked. (Gee, we wonder what part.) His crush might seem harmless at first—that is, until he buys you a white suede outfit to replace the one you borrowed from your mom in exchange for pretending to be his girlfriend.* But, if you're too chicken, we have an easier (read: passive-aggressive) way to let him down: channel the type of girl that guys *don't* go for in high school movies and you'll discourage him (and anyone, for that matter) from wanting to ever touch your boobies.

1. Wear glasses.
2. Don't be a blonde.

---

* If you don't get that this is a reference to the 1987 movie *Can't Buy Me Love*, then you need to rent it right now. Actually, finish this book first.

3. Possess a sense of humor.
4. Play sports (be aggressive, don't B-E AGGRESSIVE, because cheerleading takes you into lusted-after territory).
5. Express your extreme angst through an artistic medium such as painting, sculpture, or photography.
6. Drive a used car.
7. Listen to new wave, punk, or grrrl power music (that is, any musical group where a woman is center stage, as opposed to playing the tambourine and booty dancing in the background).
8. Excel in math, science, or auto shop.
9. Treat other girls with kindness and respect.
10. Be Ally Sheedy.

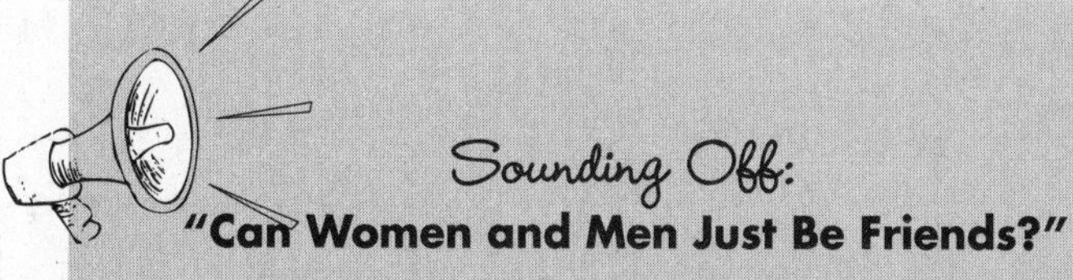

Sounding Off: "Can Women and Men Just Be Friends?"

We asked real girls the question that has launched a million romantic comedies. You might be surprised by what they had to say:

"Men and women can be just friends as long as (a.) one of them isn't secretly in love with the other or (b.) they are both so unlovable that they find solace in each other." —Mary, 28

"I guess so, although I've never had a guy friend with whom I didn't have some kind of sexual tension at one point or another." —Jeanette, 29

"Unlike most things, platonic relationships exist in real life, but not in the movies." —Jenny, 30

"There are lines that can never be crossed no matter how many cocktails you've had, and as long as both parties understand what the relationship is." —Kaitlin, 26

"Of course they can. . . . I have a lot of close guy friends."
—Christy, 28

chapter eight

BECAUSE LIKE PAULA ABDUL SAID, OPPOSITES ATTRACT

Your Unlikely Friendships

Just like tales of girl and boy friends going from platonic to erotic have inspired many a date flick, so has the notion that opposites attract (for example, the motorcycle-driving, leather-jacket-clad T-Bird getting the blond-haired, blue-eyed goody-two-shoes or the quirky redhead from the wrong side of the tracks finding love with the clean-cut Rich-y). And, just like men and women can be friends, opposites can also be drawn to each other in a totally non-lovey-dovey way. Yes, they make movies about unexpected friendship, too, but the plot usually centers on a young boy and his touching bond with an alien, a killer whale, or a dog that has wandered far, far from home. We think it's time for unlikely friendships between two human beings to get their moment in the sun.

You see, friendship isn't just about having someone around so you don't get bored on the weekends. It's also not about assembling an army of mini mes (well, technically, mini *yous*) who all list the same interests and favorite bands on their Facebook pages. It's about shared experiences, mutual respect, support, and all that other "free to be you and me" stuff.

We know that birds of a feather usually flock together, but doesn't it seem like a good idea to expand your horizons beyond those who walk and talk just like you? It takes all kinds to make the world go round and diversifying your friend portfolio will make you a more well-rounded person. Heck, you might even learn something, and isn't learning and growing and loving what life is all about (well, that, and amassing large amounts of money and material possessions in an attempt to distract ourselves from the fact that we are all gonna die anyway)?

Okay, before we make you join hands and form a friendship circle, we'll step off our soapbox and back into the world of poop jokes and pop culture. Here's the thing: your friends don't need to be as varied as the cast of *The Real World*. Actually—let's revise that, because lately, the seven strangers who are picked to live in a house are about as diverse as a wet T-shirt contest during Spring Break in Cancún (drunk, blonde, plastic and fratastic). Try this: your friends don't need to be as diverse as the cast members on the seasons of *The Real World* that preceded Las Vegas, but wouldn't you rather hang out with the Spice Girls than a bunch of Barbie dolls? Really? Not even the one who had Eddie Murphy's illegitimate child or the wacky redhead who wore the Union Jack dress? Well, then maybe you'll agree with us on this: if friends were appetizers, wouldn't you rather have Chili's Triple Dipper appetizer sampler than a measly order of mozzarella sticks? That's what we thought.

If you still need some convincing, here are some red flags that your friends are all the same.

Signs That Your Group of Friends Is Too Homogeneous

Obviously you and your friends will have many things in common. In fact, your similarities are probably what drew you together in the first place. However, unless your crew is dressing up as the chicks in that Robert Palmer video, clones aren't considered a good thing. Here's how to tell if you're just another face in your crowd and could use a little variety in your life.

- You and your friends are always mistaken for sisters.
- People have given your group some sort of childish nickname like the Fab Five.
- Your most heated conversations involve highlighting versus lowlighting your hair.
- You run out of things to talk about after fifteen minutes.
- Your version of a fashion risk is buying the same shoes as all of your friends in brown instead of black.
- You have your own made-up language and you're over the age of ten (and you're not in the band Sigur Rós).
- You voted on what the group's favorite color should be.
- No one is allowed to cut her hair without a signed permission slip.
- When asked "which celeb would play you in the movie version of your life," you all name the same person.

Typecasting: Odd Couples

Unlike members of your framily, who are so interconnected that it almost seems incestuous at times, your opposite friendships lack a common thread. There's no rhyme or reason to these bonds, since they're formed with the most unpredictable people in the most unique of ways. We guess this unpredictability is part of the fun of an oddball friendship. For example, who ever thought you'd be having coffee with a divorcée you met in one of those aerobic pole-dancing classes? Here's a closer look at some of the more likely unlikely friendships in your life and how to handle them with care.

- **The Political Adversary:** Imagine if Condoleezza Rice and Hillary Clinton could temporarily leave aside all the messiness of national security, health care, and a bunch of other pressing problems that we turn our backs on because we're too busy sticking our heads in the sand and looking for celebrity baby bumps. Without their opposing political views to ruin the fun, they would just be two wild and crazy gals—hitting up the semi-annual sale at Victoria's Secret, smelling all the lotions at Bath & Body Works, and maybe, just maybe, splitting a Cinnabon in the food court. The Political Adversary is like your own personal debate partner—you have conflicting ideas about how the world should work and aren't afraid to talk about it. However, because you're respectful of each other, your friendship is able to transcend the political divide.

  How to Deal: In order to keep the peace with the Political Adversary, you'll have to accept your differences and agree to disagree. Then, to keep the peace, choose neutral locations to hang out. And when you're feeling ballsy enough to broach a touchy subject, do it under appropriate circumstances. Her bridal shower isn't the time or place to discuss her position on the death penalty.

- **The *Tuesdays with Morrie*:** Back in high school, your mother made you volunteer at a local nursing home because it would look good on your college applications. You spent the whole time secretly hoping that the crotchety old woman in room 112, who started every conversation with "When I was your age . . ." would die and leave you millions of dollars that no one knew she had. Now that you're a mature adult, you've grown to respect your elders and even befriend them. Take, for instance, your *Tuesdays with Morrie* friend. She's older and wiser and can teach you invaluable life lessons, like which STDs can be treated with antibiotics and which can't. She might even be the same age as your parents, but unlike the people who brought you into this world (Hi Mom and Dad!) you actually seek out her advice about all sorts of personal matters. In this society, which values youth and smooth, expressionless foreheads over wisdom and aging gracefully, the *Tuesdays with Morrie* is a sign of hope that once you reach her age, you can still be pretty damn cool.

  How to Deal: While your older friend can offer you all sorts of insight, perspective, and other Mr. Miyagi–type wisdom, that doesn't mean you should take everything she says as gospel, especially if she was your age back when people took quaaludes like they were vitamins and wouldn't let something like a pregnancy get in the way of their after-dinner smoke and scotch.

- **The *Adventures in Babysitting*:** Just like it's beneficial to make friends who are older than you, there's something to be said for taking on the mentor role for today's youth. No, we don't mean telling your eight-year-old niece how to work her feminine charms on the cute boy in her social studies class. We're thinking more along the lines of having lunch with the intern at your office who always compliments your sense of style, laughs at all of the lame jokes you make during meetings, and has a picture of Prince Harry as her screen saver. Your *Adventures in Babysitting* friend entertains you with her hilarious stories of crazy hookups and psychotic roommates and also reminds you that your early twenties weren't so great after all.

How to Deal: Before you get all Yoda on her ass just because you proofread her résumé and were able to talk her out of taking that sixth-floor walk-up apartment with the bathtub in the kitchen, realize that you can also learn a lot from your *Adventures in Babysitting* friend. She can show you how to upload a video onto YouTube, tell you which bands are cool, and explain the appeal of *High School Musical*. Just remember: after you spend a night slamming Jägermeister shots with *Adventures in Babysitting* and the rest of her barely legal crew and are left bedridden for forty-eight hours, you have no one to blame but yourself. You're older, wiser, and should've known better than to go drinking on a school night. Now go take a couple of aspirins and drink some Gatorade to replenish those electrolytes that you threw up last night. And this morning. And, also, this afternoon. Unfortunately, they have yet to make a sports drink that replenishes your youth.

- **The Advanced Stage:** You may have met her when you

were both in a similar place in your lives. Then one day, without any warning, she says, "We're looking at townhouses" or "We're trying to get pregnant," thus becoming the Advanced Stage friend. She's light-years ahead of you in maturity and has one, some, or all of the following: a husband, an ex-husband, a mortgage, life insurance, a dog, or a child. As a result, the Advanced Stage introduces you to fascinating things you've only read about, like wedding registries, prenups, Home Depot, and breast pumps.

How to Deal: As fascinated as you may be about the Advanced Stage's life, try not to overuse the phrase "I can't believe you have a [insert grownup thing]" when you're around her. Trust us, she doesn't need you to remind her that she's the mother of triplets, and she can just as easily say to you, "I can't believe you still sleep on a futon."

✦ **The History Lesson:** Once upon of time, life was simple and you had everything in common with her, including a love of My Little Pony, the color pink, and bubblegum-flavored lip gloss. Fast forward a decade or two, through a flurry of psychosexual development, life experience, and ever-changing hairstyles, and the two of you couldn't be a more unlikely pairing. Thanks to your shared past, though, you've managed to transcend your differences and remain friends. She's your History Lesson, a helpful reminder that so much changes, yet so much stays the same. (You both still love pink.)

How to Deal: Make the effort to stay in touch and understand that you and the History Lesson have a bond that will last forever, but you may drift in and out of each other's lives.

Friend in Focus: The Yin to Your Yang—Your Polar Opposite Friend

What's Her Deal: You say "to-may-to" and she says "to-mah-to." You say "Man-oh-lo" and she says, "Why in the world would you spend that much on a pair of shoes?" Your theme song is "Shiny Happy People," while her high school nickname was Daria. She's a type-A insomniac with a Red Bull addiction and you're an easy-going kabbalah follower who likes to journal. Okay, so you and Your Polar Opposite are about as close to twins as Danny DeVito and the Governator, but somehow, your mismatched friendship just works. Experts have a very experty explanation for unusual pairings: We're drawn to people who possess whatever qualities or personality traits we lack. Research is all well and good, but you and your Polar Opposite Friend might just be another example of two unlikely ingredients coming together to make a delightful duo, like celery and peanut butter and Michael Jackson and Bubbles.

How You Meet: Since you probably wouldn't gravitate toward each other in a normal social setting, you and Your Polar Opposite Friend bond in an arranged situation. Possible meeting places include locked up in a room of your "peers" while on jury duty (she's the only other person who isn't a retiree); during your freshman year of college (you were randomly paired up as roommates); and at work (you share workspace in the pod city).

Symptoms of Your Polar Opposite Friend

1. It's Puzzling: Opposites may attract, but it takes more than intrigue and fascination with the unknown to keep an odd couple together. (Otherwise, Christie Brinkley would still be married to Billy Joel.) As we mentioned earlier, we seek out contrasting personality types as a way to compensate in the areas where we fall short. This means your Polar Opposite is like a missing puzzle piece that brings to the table whatever you can't (and vice versa). So, if you're a wallflower, you'd want to befriend a social butterfly. If you're a pessimist, you'd look for an optimist. And if you're a big ho, then a born-again virgin would fill that hole, so to speak.

2. Fundamental Similarities: Beneath your superficial differences (like hair color and taste in music), you and your Polar Opposite Friend have similar core values (like honesty, respect, and kindness toward others). But don't worry if you disagree on major things like finances, religion, and child-rearing, since you're not judging her as a potential romantic partner.

3. Alone Time: It's not that you're ashamed of or embarrassed by your Polar Opposite Friend, but she doesn't exactly fit in with the rest of your friends and you don't exactly fit in with hers. As a result, the two of you spend a lot of alone time together. Don't look at this as a bad thing, though, since it allows you to get to know each other in an intensive and contained way—kind of like lab partners or prison roommates.

4. Push the Envelope: One of the best parts of your friendship is that you challenge each other to step out of your comfort zones and do things that you've never done before. For example: she takes you shopping at mass retail stores like Target (a six-pack of socks for $5.99? score!) and you get her to try quinoa with grilled tofu. It's a win-win situation. (Well, maybe not so much judging by her reaction to your favorite vegetarian dish.)

Why You Love Your Polar Opposite Friend: Because you aren't carbon copies of each other, conversations with her are always far from boring.

Example: Even her views about Britney Spears's infamous VMA performance were enlightening.

Why She Sometimes Irks You: There are some things that you will never fully understand about her.

Example: She thinks Julia Roberts looked best as a blonde.

How to Be a Better Friend to Your Polar Opposite: It's one thing to make fun of her for owning every season of *Dr. Quinn, Medicine Woman* on DVD, but tread lightly when it comes to touchier subjects. We're sure she doesn't appreciate it that you make it a point to constantly tell her how incredibly creepy you think cats are when you know full well that she owns two of them and has a picture of them as her cell wallpaper.

How Your Friendship Will Fare: Good, considering the fact that as we move through different stages in our lives, we change and so do our tastes. (Remember how you used to hate olives, but now you love them?) As we grow up, we may realize that some friends who are the same on the surface actually have very different values.

Where Your Polar Opposite Will Be in Ten Years: Doing the exact opposite of what you're doing (duh).

We Go Together Like . . .
Famous Unlikely Friendships

Some of the best celebrity buds are also some of the most unusual, such as four women with seemingly nothing in common (other than an alarmingly high number of sexual partners), a neurotic comic book geek and the bad boy from Chino and, of course, a man and his monkey. Here, our favorite on- and offscreen "who would've thunk it" friends.

- The *Sex and the City* quartet
- Katie Holmes and Victoria Beckham
- Michael Jackson and Bubbles (yes, we name-dropped MJ and his right-hand chimp earlier, but so what?)
- Michael Jackson and Elizabeth Taylor
- Michael Jackson and Macaulay Culkin
- David Bowie and Bing Crosby
- Diddy and Ashton
- Seth Cohen and Ryan Atwood
- Bill Clinton and George H. W. Bush
- Chris Tucker and Jackie Chan
- Napoleon Dynamite and Pedro Sanchez

It's the Little Things: Your Common Ground

With all this talk about the glaring differences between you and your Polar Opposite, it's easy to forget that she's the only person you know who agrees with you on the following:

- R. Kelly's *Trapped in the Closet,* Chapters 1 through Whatever, is the *Carmen* of our time.
- Bravo and Court TV are the only channels on television worth watching.
- Casey is and always has been the hotter Affleck brother.
- Forever 21: It's not just for twenty-one-year-olds.
- Laughter might be the best medicine, but Domino's Thin Crust Pizza comes in a close second.
- Airplane food is kind of good.
- Tupac is alive.
- So is Biggie.
- And Keith Richards.

Fantasy Opposite Friendships

Forget fantasy football. Below are some ultimate friend pair-ups. Imagine how the world would be a better, or at least more entertaining, place if these duos actually existed.

- **Musical Duet:** Celine Dion and Kanye West
- **Politics:** Dick Cheney and Stephen Colbert
- **TV Talk Show:** Larry King and Tyra Banks
- **Buddy Movie Duo:** Borat and Vince Vaughn
- **Literary Duo:** Carrie Bradshaw and Stephen King
- **Celebutarian:** Bono and Paris Hilton
- **Bonnie and Clyde 2.0:** The Unabomber and Lisa "Diaper Astronaut" Nowak
- **Culinary Partners:** Emeril and White Castle
- **Business Tycoons:** That douche who founded *Girls Gone Wild* and Martha Stewart (only because you know she would beat his ass down)

chapter nine

• • • • • • • • • •

OUTERSPACE

Lunch Dates, Drinking Buddies, and Various Other Acquaintances

Ever since preschool, we've been taught that sharing is caring. When it comes to double chocolate brownie sundaes, anything made by Fisher-Price, and online porn, we couldn't agree more. On the other hand, sharing ceases to be caring when it involves dumping your hopes, fears, secrets, and personal problems on anyone who will listen. T.M.I. was once relegated to conversations with your doctor or your nutty great-aunt who is too old to care what other people think about her anymore. Now it's become socially acceptable and even encouraged as a way to bond with friends (or millions of strangers via YouTube). The frequency of your bowel movements? *(Sure, let's talk about it!)* Your preferred sexual position? *(I'm dying to know!)* You wax it all off down there? *(Me too!)*

Luckily, there's a place you can go when you need to escape T.M.I. Welcome to Outerspace, the furthermost reaches of your social stratosphere, where, for the most part, people haven't stopped being polite and started getting real. Reserved for gym buddies, neighbors, and various other people who don't know your middle name, the acquaintances in your Outerspace won't ever replace your closest friends, but they make your everyday world a smaller and friendlier place. They also contribute to your life in some invaluable ways, like padding the Evite list for your birthday party, keeping you company at the gym, picking up your mail when you're out of town, and helping you network professionally. And, you never know, with a little TLC, today's acquaintance can become tomorrow's friend with whom you're free to share T.M.I.

Know Your Audience

As hard as this may be to accept, trust us when we tell you that not everyone in your social sphere needs to know everything about you. Here we tell you how to filter information depending on whom you're talking to.

Topic	Acquaintance	Close Friend
Mental health	You're switching from regular to decaf.	You're switching from Zoloft to Lexapro.
Political views	You're a liberal.	The last time you voted for a president was during your high school student council elections.
Personal grooming	You're hair color is from a box.	The carpet doesn't match the drapes . . . that is if you had any carpet left after last week's waxing appointment.
Romantic life	Looking for Mr. Right	Banging Mr. Right Now
Diet and exercise	You're on a low-carb diet and take yoga.	You're on those new diet pills and hope that you don't shit yourself during yoga.

Typecasting: Friendly Types

Think of the Outerspace as a combination of the people in your neighborhood and your acquaintances. Read on for tips for dealing with these friends lite.

- **The Third Wheel:** Your relationship with the Third Wheel is completely dependant upon a mutual friend. When you all hang out as a trio, the chemistry's just right, the good times roll, and the conversations flow. Then, as soon as you and the Third Wheel have to interact with each other minus the presence of your shared pal, things falls apart like an Oreo cookie without the cream filling. Perhaps three really is the magic number when it comes to this friendship.

  How to Deal: If you want to get to know the Third Wheel a bit better, just give it some time for a deeper friendship to develop. On the other hand, if you and the Third Wheel work best in a trio setting, that's okay, too. After all, what would a BLT be without the bacon or Bell Biv Devoe be without the Biv?
- **The Friendly Neighbor:** It helps to maintain good relations with the people who live around you. Not only is it the nice thing to do, but it's comforting to know that the Friendly Neighbor's got your back and you've got hers: You sign for her FedEx packages while she's at work and she feeds your cat while you're away on vacation. Living in close quarters gives you a sense of semi-familiarity with the people who semi-share your space, which makes for strangely intimate relationships with your neighbors. Hav-

ing the Friendly Neighbor in your life helps alleviate your fear that you will choke on a Hot Pocket and no one, with the exception of your cat, will notice that you're gone. You just wish your walls were a bit thicker so you didn't have to hear your Friendly Neighbor and her boyfriend going bump in the night (and sometimes in the morning, too).

How to Deal: The key to a healthy relationship with your Friendly Neighbor is striking a balance between pleasant and politely aloof. No one wants to have a nosy Nancy dropping by her front door unannounced at all hours. If you want to add more friendly neighbors to your life, remember that a smile goes a long way, but a juicy tidbit about the landlord's creepy, deadbeat son who lives in the basement apartment goes even further.

✦ **The Professional Contact:** When it comes to annoying office buzzword mumbo jumbo, the phrase "networking" is right up there with "thinking outside the box" and "downsizing." As unnatural as it seems to attend contrived industry parties and cocktail hours with the sole purpose of meeting new people that you can use, sometimes the networking thing actually works out and you exchange business cards with a very cool, calm, and connected person. With the Professional Contact, you scratch her back and she scratches yours, but you actually like and trust each other enough to go out and grab a drink.

How to Deal: While you should definitely have fun with your Professional Contact, don't ever forget that you need to remain at least semi-professional around her. No one wants to hire a girl who had one too many glasses of

Chardonnay and then had to excuse herself to vomit in the unisex bathroom.

- **The Party Girl:** You have fair-weather friends and then you have the Party Girl, who, in terms of climate conditions, is more of a San Diego friend (always in the seventies and sunny). Like a no-strings-attached fling, you call her whenever you want to hit the town and do something that you'll probably regret in the morning.

  How to Deal: Even though you always have a great time with the Party Girl (otherwise her name would be something like "Sits at Home and Watches *Matlock* Girl"), you tend to overlook her when it comes to daytime activities. But most likely she's just as fun to hang out with when the only shots you're doing are of espresso.

- **The Gym Friend:** She knows what you look like with your clothes off and she didn't even have to buy you dinner first, and you've heard her moan and groan and you don't even know her last name. This is how it goes with the Gym Friend. You've seen each other at your worst (sweaty and without makeup), yet you keep your relationship polite (exchanging niceties, workout advice, and other benign chatter). Your quasi-friendship exists in a world of free weights, spinning classes, and elliptical machines and far away from life on the "outside" where men don't stand around and flex for each other unless they're looking for more than a workout buddy.

  How to Deal: If you feel the need to have a conversation with the Gym Friend in the locker room, for the love of all that's holy, please put on some clothes first. Nobody wants to see that.

Friend in Focus: Your Girl Crush

The Friend Who Sets Your Heart A-Flutter in a Nonsexual Way (Not That There Would Be Anything Wrong with That)

What's Her Deal: Men want to be with her and women want to be her. She's your Girl Crush—a combination of beauty, brains, balls, and bodaciousness that sets your heart a-flutter. Don't get us wrong. It's not like you want to marry her or anything. You just think she's really cool. Plus, she has the prettiest hair and you'd really like to brush it—in the most nonsexual way possible.

You admire everything about the Girl Crush, from her ability to rock high-waisted jeans and create the perfect smoky eye to the fact that she is in a knitting club and spends two Sundays per month delivering food for Meals on Wheels. She's even better than Laurie Miller, who was a senior when you were a freshman in high school. She drove a Jeep Wrangler, had a boyfriend who was in college, and wore Prescriptives Calyx (not that you ever got close enough to her to catch a whiff, you just overheard her talking about it during study hall).

How You Meet: You and the Girl Crush exchange knowing glances from across the bar at a mutual friend-of-a-friend-of-a-friend's birthday get-together. Before you even get a chance to talk to her, you feel relieved that someone else is having as bad of a time as you are. Desperate for a conversation that doesn't begin with "So, you come here often?" you weave your way to her side of the room through the throngs of sweaty bodies dry-humping to late nineties hip-hop. You compliment her turquoise tights (you could never pull those off!) and make your introductions. Not surprisingly, you and Your Girl Crush immediately hit if off, punctuating your conversations with multiple shrieks of "Ohmygod" and "Me too" as you discover how much you have in common.

When you've had enough of the party, your Girl Crush suggests making a break for it and hitting an after-hours club across town where she occasionally iPod DJs Brit pop and indie rock. (That's so cool!) Afterward, the two of you hit the twenty-four-hour diner, share a plate of disco fries, and swap life stories. You feel giddy with glee that you were finally allowed to sit at the cool kids' lunch table.

Symptoms of Your Girl Crush

1. Jill of All Trades: The Girl Crush is everywoman: fashionista, worker bee, It girl, humanitarian, world traveler—the list goes on and on. She's the only one in your yoga class who can do Crow Pose, plus she never has camel toe. She's seen and done it all with finesse, confidence, and ease. Since you consider flossing your teeth after you brush to be a great achievement, you go back and forth between feeling awestruck and inadequate around your Girl Crush.

2. It Goes Both Ways: Believe it or not, often the feeling is mutual and the Girl Crush is just as enamored with you (OMG, right?!). While you're agonizing over how to ask her for her phone number, she's actually wondering the same thing. This revelation is the equivalent of that moment when you're on date number three with a guy you really like and he tells you that he's taken his profile off the online dating site that you met him on and hopes that you'll do the same. It's an intoxicating mix of excitement, relief, and disbelief that someone this amazing feels the same way about you.

3. Everything Old Is New Again: You haven't had such an intense rush of adrenaline since your parents said that you could go to the mall by yourself. When the Girl Crush invites you out for coffee, you try to act nonchalant ("You like coffee?! Me too!") but inside you're totally freaking out. You spend an hour getting dressed (should you go with jeans or something trendy like a bubble skirt?) and brush up on an array of current events should she ask your opinion on anything from celebrity gossip to the political unrest in the Middle East. Even the most mundane of activities like going to the movies becomes as adventure—you can't wait to find out if she puts butter on her popcorn or if she likes Reese's Pieces. And, if she likes Reese's Pieces mixed into popcorn, it's love. (Don't knock it till you try it. It's yummy.)

4. Idol Worship: Like a real romantic attraction, part of the excitement is that you don't know her as well as you know your other friends, so you fill in the blanks with the idealized vision you have in your head. For example, you just assume that someone as sophisticated as she must've been born in a big city, where she probably had really cool parents who encouraged her to read grown-up books and maybe even smoked pot with her on occasion. You've never been to her apartment, but you just know that it's straight out of one of those hip, young decorating magazines with quirky vintage flea-market finds and something totally chic like a pink couch. The only problem with all this speculating is that inevitably the reality won't live up to the fantasy and you'll be crushed when you find out that she's from Nowheresville and all of her furniture is from Ikea—just like yours.

Why You Love Her: Well, besides the obvious (her amazing blond highlights and her knowledge of all the words to "It's the End of the World As We Know It (And I Feel Fine)," not just "Leonard Bernstein!") the Girl Crush is everything you aspire to be one day: independent, ambitious, and, well, really pretty.

Example: Hearing about her recent trip to Costa Rica, where she stayed in an eco-lodge and learned how to surf, motivates you to book the vacation to Reykjavik that you've been talking about for months.

Why She Sometimes Irks You: It's not so much that she as a person has flaws, but that the nature of the relationship causes you anxiety, since the slightest shift in her mood or tone can send you into a panic that she's so over you.

Example: When she waited twenty-seven hours to return your e-mail, you made an emergency appointment with your therapist so she could talk you down from you insecurity-induced anxiety attack.

How to Be a Better Friend to the Girl Crush: We know that it's hard to believe that a goddess like her has fat days and gets zits, but once in a while you should let her get down from her pedestal so she can go to the bathroom (yes, she does that, too).

How Your Friendship Will Fare: You cannot in fact have an actual friendship with the Girl Crush until the wooing period ends. And assuming that the flame doesn't extinguish for you once you realize that she's a regular person, a lifelong friendship can develop (see "An Affair to Remember," below).

Where Your Girl Crush Will Be in Ten Years: Scaling mountains in Mongolia, drinking Darjeeling tea in New Delhi, or opening a vintage store in Williamsburg.

An Affair to Remember: The Life Cycle of a Girl Crush

It begins with infatuation, gets stronger with every laugh you share, and can end with tears. Here, how a girl crush can either go from lust to love or can be over before you can say, "I swear I'm not a stalker."

The Beginning: At first you're intrigued by her physical appearance (what lip gloss is that?) but once you actually talk to her, it's the girl behind the perfect shade of pink that makes your heart flutter. She also makes your palms sweat and gets you more hot and bothered than the underage boys in the Abercrombie & Fitch catalog. You start emulating everything, from her sense of style to the way she drinks her coffee (black, of course). Your friends roll their eyes when you reference your Girl Crush for the umpteenth time in a conversation, but you can't help it—you've got it bad. (Perhaps even worse than Usher in the video where he rolls around in his bed wearing only white boxer shorts and a diamond necklace.)

The Middle: At some point (usually after your third glass of Pinot Grigio) you confess your true feelings to your Girl Crush and it is this moment that will forever alter the dynamics of the relationship. As we mentioned earlier, there's a good chance that your love won't go unrequited and she's just as enamored of you. However, before you get matching airbrushed T-shirts with your name plus her name in a heart, keep in mind that, sadly, not all crushes are mutual and not every Girl Crush thinks it's cute to have a Mini Me. If she recoils at your proclamation of love, try not to cry, plead, or refuse to let go of her leg as she tries to run away from you. Clearly she's not worthy of your affection and you should put the cork from the bottle of wine you shared in a shoebox under your bed along with the lock of hair you snipped when she was sleeping.

The End: Assuming that your Girl Crush didn't take out a restraining order, the end can actually be the beginning (deep, we know) since once everyone's feelings are on the table, you can get on with the business of being normal friends.

Signs You're Ready to Take It to the Next Level

You've hung out with her numerous times, met a few of her friends, and even know her favorite color. So is she still an acquaintance or can you call her a friend? Here's how to tell if your relationship has qualified for an upgrade:

- You've stopped spell-checking your e-mails to her and you now sign them "xoxo."
- You text message each other over the holidays.
- You've gotten wasted together.
- You've gone number two in her apartment.
- You no longer include a reference after her name—such as Julie from the gym—when talking about her.
- You've made a "Fourth Meal" run to Taco Bell together.
- You've borrowed an item of clothing from her.
- You can say "remember when" and not refer to something that happened last week.
- You let her pluck a hair from your chin.

Top Celeb Girl Crushes, Arranged Alphabetically by Category

If you're lacking in real-life girl crushes, here are some famous really cool women who are worthy of your affections:

- Comediennes: Tina Fey, Amy Poehler, Sarah Silverman
- Fictional but Fierce: Jem, Scarlett O'Hara, O-Ren Ishii
- Gay Icons: Kylie Minogue, Madonna, Elton John
- Girls with Balls: Mia Hamm, Maria Sharapova, Jennie Finch
- Gone but Far from Forgotten: June Carter Cash, Tammy Faye Bakker, Jacqueline Kennedy Onassis
- Good Girls: Mandy Moore, Kelly Clarkson, Amanda Bynes
- Hip-Hop Hotties: Rihanna, Kelis, Salt-N-Pepa
- Historical Hotties: Jane Austen, Annie Oakley, Rosie the Riveter
- Humanitarians: Angelina Jolie, Melinda Gates, Queen Rania
- Indie Ingenues: Parker Posey, Neko Case, Kim Gordon
- Like Fine Wine: Iman, Helen Mirren, Sophia Loren
- Living Legends: Dolly Parton, Tina Turner, Emmylou Harris
- Out and Proud: Ellen DeGeneres, Joan Jett, k.d. lang
- Politicos: Margaret Thatcher, Eleanor Roosevelt, Sandra Day O'Connor
- Quirky Cool: Zooey Deschanel, M.I.A., Chloë Sevigny
- Survivors: Martha Stewart, Hillary Clinton, Elizabeth Taylor
- Tough on the Outside: Kat Von D, Xena: Warrior Princess, Amy Winehouse
- Totally Eighties: Molly Ringwald, Apollonia, Cindy Mancini

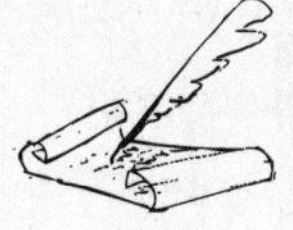

Ms. Friendship Manners

Dear Ms. Friendship Manners,

I have a problem with double-booking myself. Here's a recent example: I had made plans with a friend to go to dinner and a movie on a Friday night. It promised to be a fun time—not wild and crazy, but fun nonetheless. However, another friend called me up right after I made those plans and told me that she had an extra ticket to see one of my most favorite bands ever. In my excitement, I accepted her offer. When I realized my mistake, I felt torn. I really wanted to go see the show but I didn't want it to seem like I was blowing off my dinner-and-a-movie date for something better. So, rather than tell her the truth, I feigned a nasty cough and spent the evening at the concert, feeling edgy and paranoid that I would get caught in my lie. In the future, how should I handle situations like these?

I'm not a liar, I swear,
Juggling in Jacksonville

Dear Juggling,

My, my, what a full dance card you have. The general rule of thumb regarding making and breaking plans with friends is this: first come, first served. In other words, if you make a scheduling boo-boo and double-book yourself, the polite thing to do is to go with the first obligation. In your case, it sounded like you accidentally-on-purpose made plans with another friend. Ms. Friendship Manners wishes that you would have come clean and explained the situation to everyone involved, rather than pretending to have the croup and potentially hurting someone's feelings with your tall tales. As long as you don't make a habit of ditching, a good friend would understandably accept a rain check if something monumental landed on your plate, such as the chance to see your favorite band or go on a date with your dream man. (Back in her single-swinging, Bartles-and-Jaymes-sipping days, you better believe that Ms. Friendship Manners would clear her calendar if she was presented with the opportunity to share an evening with Mr. Tom Selleck.)

Here is a final tip for a busy woman such as yourself: Get yourself a day planner.

Part Three
That's What Friends Are (and Aren't) For

Make ups, breakups, and drama, oh my! This may sound like the latest episode of *One Tree Hill,* but this is actually the part of *Friend or Frenemy?* where we cut the crap and offer you some practical advice on how to develop more meaningful, rewarding friendships. We've already given you a guide to the friends (and frenemies) in your social circle, so here's how to make it all work. Oh, who are we kidding? That would be like saying we read *The New Yorker*, as opposed to just flipping through and looking at the cartoons.

chapter ten

BALANCING FRIENDSHIP AND COUPLEDOM

After countless disastrous dates and a few affairs to forget, you've finally met your Prince Charming. Or maybe you're on the other end of the relationship spectrum: single and ready to mingle. No matter what the state of your love life—happily attached or as footloose and fancy-free as young Kevin Bacon when he danced away his anger like no one was watching in that giant warehouse—balancing friendships with matters of the heart can be trickier than walking across a tightrope in stilettos.

By now you should have realized that this is a *relating* rather than a dating book, but we can't talk about friendship without touching upon the challenges of integrating romantic relationships into your social circle.

Maybe it's the pheromones or maybe it's because we're taught that we should do whatever it takes to fulfill our heart's desires, but love can make otherwise rational people do irrational things, like write bad poetry, dress up with their significant others as pairs of fuzzy dice for Halloween, and bicker with friends. It doesn't get easier with age, either, because romantic relationships only become more intense, paving the way for a lifetime of uncomfortable social situations.

For example: What happens when you are the only unattached girl in your group of friends, or what if you are the only one who has a steady Friday night date? Why do some people feel the need to make assumptions, like if you're single you must be lonely or if you're "married off" you no longer need friends? Can't we all just get along?

Of course, it doesn't have to be this way. The key to happiness in your romantic and friendly relations is balance. Some people do this naturally, while others need a little more help. In order to better serve you (and give you a kick in the bum if you need it), we decided to tackle the topic of relationship feng shui from two viewpoints: the single and the coupled. Which one are you?

One, Singular Sensation: What to Do When You're the Last Single Girl Standing in Your Group of Friends

Throughout most of your life, you and your friends have moved at a similar pace, hitting the major milestones like your first period, first bra, and first real job around the same time. Regarding relationships, though, there comes a time when some people sprint like the hare toward an imaginary finish line, while others take things in stride and ease on down the road of life like a tortoise.

When you're in the latter group, it probably seems like all of your friends went from available to off the market overnight and you're the only one who isn't settling down, shacking up, or registering for $90 wineglasses—you know, the basics. You're happy with yourself, but you can't fight off this irrational fear that you're the odd woman out and your weekend plans, which were once filled with spontaneous outings with the girls, are now going to dry up because everyone is hanging out with their significant others or consumed by bridal showers, bachelorette parties, and, of course, weddings, weddings, and more weddings.

It's not that you're bitter (after all, who doesn't want to commit hours of their time and hundreds of their dollars in the name of someone else's love), but perhaps you're overreacting just a little? It's okay to feel a teeny tiny bit of resentment if you've just gone through a disastrous breakup and the entire known universe appears to be happily attached at the hip, mocking your heartache. Those *woe is me* feelings should disappear with time. And it's okay to feel more than a teeny tiny bit of resentment if some of your attached friends, who at one point seemed like they were totally normal, suddenly take it upon themselves to make you as "happy" as they are, urging their boyfriends and husbands to set you up with anyone who is "cute and single," which is code for "single." (Like you'd ever think that the ultimate catch is some aging frat boy whose nickname is Shotgun, given for his world-renowned beer chugging skills.)

While you're busy playing yourself the world's tiniest violin, don't forget one of the Friend Commandments: *Thou shalt not covet thy friend's life*. Your attached friends may be experiencing their own bout of "grass is always greener" syndrome. Why else do you think they grill you for all the dirty details of your latest hook up? Duh, they're living vicariously through you.

Here's the bottom line: If you really are the only unattached woman in your social circle and are bothered by it, you should live la vida solo to the best of your ability. Seek out some new friends to add to the mix, eat a bag of Tostitos Hint of Lime chips for dinner, watch Drew Barrymore movies all night without having to explain to someone why you like them so much. Also, don't forget that your coupled friends are, um, still your friends. They just added another dimension to their lives. Friendship is a two-way street, so why don't you reach out and try to incorporate your bestie's new man into your social circle—even if he does chew with his mouth open.

Ointment for Those Burning Personal Questions

You're perfectly happy with your single girl status, but some other people will find a way to make you feel as lonely and desperate as possible by asking you intrusive questions about your love life. Ironically, those inquiring minds aren't your close friends or your family (except for your nana, who's ninety-one, so you let it slide), but instead, they are acquaintances, semi-friends on the fringes of your social circle, or even total strangers. Why do people do this? There are two possibilities: they lack tact and are just clueless or, more likely, they are insecure and want to question others in order to make themselves feel better about their own life choices. Our advice: the next time someone puts you on the spot with a totally inappropriate question, offer up an equally inappropriate answer. Here is a little cheat sheet to get you started.

Prying Question	Your Appropriately Inappropriate Response
Are you seeing anyone special?	No, but I hear that your husband is.
Why aren't you dating anyone?	Because it's so much more fun sleeping around.
I know this great guy. Can I set you two up?	Do you know any great girls?
I heard you broke up with your boyfriend. What happened?	He wasn't into anal—total deal breaker, right?
But don't you want kids one day?	Thanks to people like you there doesn't seem to be a shortage of them.
How is someone like you still single?	Probably because my standards are slightly higher than yours.

When "I" Becomes "We": How to Be a Girlfriend and a Girl Friend

Since the moment you laid half-closed eyes on each other at the bar, you and Mr. Perfect have been joined at the lips. Every conversation you have with your friends begins with, "Ohmygod, did I tell you guys the really cute thing he said to me?" You just can't help gushing about how amazing he is, how in love you are, and how you have so much in common because he also loves dogs and wants to one day own a house on a lake.

Your friends couldn't be happier for you. After all, they were the ones who spent countless hours listening to you talk about your romantic woes, assuring you that you would find a nice, normal guy, then holding your hand when that nice, normal guy dumped you on your ass. Their happiness will be short-lived, though, if all you do is go on and on about your relationship or, worse, neglect them completely so you can spend even more time with your boyfriend. We know it's tempting to hole up in your love nest during the honeymoon period of your relationship, but there comes a time when you need to remove your face from his and return to the regularly scheduled program known as your life. (And for crissakes, wipe that postsex glow off your face, young lady).

Even if you can successfully maintain equilibrium between your two worlds (and, if you're struggling to do so, see "Juggling Act" on page 173) it's not always going to be smooth sailing. You'll probably feel a twinge of guilt when you can't make it to an impromptu brunch or dinner with the girls because you have plans with your guy. It's tough when you want to be in two places at once but even attempting to do so will only result in driving yourself crazy. You're better off accepting that being in a relationship means compromise, but not compromising yourself.

It Takes More Than Two to Make a Thing Go Right: The World of "Couple Friends"

If you're one of the only attached women in your groups of friends, it makes sense that you would want to expand your social horizons a bit. Your single friends, who may be good for the occasional night on the town, are less than enthusiastic about being the third wheel, so together, in your matching medium wash bootcut jeans, you and your man venture into the world of couple friends, aka "dating as a duo."

Choosing couple friends resembles sorority rush. You check out all of the options (see "Double Trouble" on page 172), find one that best fits your personality (and level of attractiveness), and then hope that the feeling is mutual.

That being said, it's best to make some new couple friends through your respective jobs and mutual acquaintances. "Couples dating" is a lot like real dating: you have to put yourselves out there—not your regular selves, of course, but your most witty and charming selves. Before your first big "date" (dinner at a nice but not overly stuffy restaurant), you and your boyfriend prep each other. He reminds you that not everyone considers collecting handbags a hobby and you threaten to kick his shins under the table if he eats the garnish or talks when his mouth is full of food during dinner.

Also, just like traditional dating, despite your best efforts, there's always a chance that you and your prospective couples friends won't hit it off. Resist the urge to blame it on the off-color joke your boyfriend made or that after drinking an entire bottle of wine you asked the girl if she had a weave in her hair. Sometimes, shit happens.

Eventually, you and your man will find a couple that you click with. Hopefully, the four of you will end up happily ever after like an episode of *Friends*, but if one of your relationships were to end, things could get dicey. Custody should be awarded to whoever brought the couple in—did he know the guy from work or did you meet her from the gym? If you made friends with them as a couple, you'll have to carry on separate friendships. Actually, we'll leave this one alone, because breakups and friend custody could take up a whole other book.

Double Trouble: Types of Couples

In your quest to find another duo to do all kinds of fun couples things with (and disco is dead, so we don't mean partner swapping) you may encounter some rather colorful twosomes. Consider this chart a cheat sheet to what kinds of pairs are out there just waiting to be your new besties.

	The Train-wrecks	The Richie Riches	The Social Activists	The Beautiful People	The Hipsters
Favorite conversation topic	Things you can swallow or snort	Real-estate investments	Global warming	The best facial line fillers	Gentrification of the neighborhood
Hobbies	Bailing each other out of jail	Looking at properties	"Activism"	Working out	Critiquing art but doing nothing to contribute to it
Where they met	At Promises in Malibu	The country club where both of their families are members	A WTO protest	On a catalog shoot	At an independent record store
Vacation plans	Vegas, baby!	Aspen	Habitat for Humanity	South Beach	Anywhere the Travel Channel hasn't featured
Dirty secret	She always fakes it.	The Beamer is a lease.	They're addicted to Starbucks.	Her boobs are fake and so are his calves.	His parents are doctors and she has a trust fund.

	The Train-wrecks	The Richie Riches	The Social Activists	The Beautiful People	The Hipsters
Identifying features	His and hers tattoos	His and hers diamond Rolexes	His and hers hemp sneakers	His and hers veneers	His and hers asym-metrical haircuts
Drink of choice	Jack Daniels	Pellegrino	Wheatgrass shots	Red Bull and vodka	Pabst Blue Ribbon
They smell like . . .	K-Y Warm-ing Liquid	The interior of a new BMW	A pungent blend of patchouli and body odor	The self-tanner section of Sephora	A "vintage" shirt from the Salva-tion Army

Juggling Act: Balancing Your Friendships and Your Romantic Relationships

Let's be honest, it's easy (read: lazy) to pick up and move to couple-land, a place where your significant other takes on the role of best friend and your couple friends are the only supporting cast you have. But we don't have to tell you how bad it is to sacrifice your friendships for your relationship, right? Here's how to keep the peace among the most important people in your life.

- **Mix it up:** Separation of church and state is good for things like, um, church and state, but it shouldn't apply to your boyfriend and your friends. We're not saying he should join you and your BFF for weekly mani-pedis, but it might be a good idea to let everyone mingle together once in awhile. Invite the girls to his place for drinks or bring him along to lunch or coffee (just give your friends the heads-up first). The more they all hang out, the more comfortable they'll feel around him. Plus, he'll see how important they are to you.

- **Know when to shut yer yap.** We know that T.M.I. is imbedded in a girl's DNA, but there is such a thing as oversharing when it comes to your relationship. While it's good to keep your friends in the loop about your life, they only need to know so much. What he gave you for your birthday? Spill it sister. The first time he said "I love you"? They'll love to hear the story. He sings show tunes during sex? For your ears only and possibly the ears of a couples' therapist.
- **That being said, don't leave your friends in the dark.** If we just made you paranoid that you're blabbing too much to your friends, don't zip your lips up completely. Unless you have a good reason for keeping them in the dark about your relationship (for example, he's married with children, you home wrecker) being secretive about it will only make them think that you have something to hide.

Ladies First: Making Amends When You're the Ditcher

You swore that you'd never be *that* girl, and by *that* girl we mean the Ditcher, the frenemy who finds a new love interest, buys two tickets to paradise, and leaves her friends in the dust because she's too busy being all smoochie woochie to realize that she and her love muffin aren't the last people left on Earth. (Understand that the Ditcher is an extreme case who is not to be confused with someone who, you know, has a significant other in her life with whom she enjoys spending time. Instead, she gets wrapped up in romantic relationships in an unhealthy way and puts all of her social and emotional eggs in one basket, so to speak.) It's one thing to occasionally double-book yourself, but it's quite another to be so immersed in your relationship that you lose contact with everyone but your significant other. Read on to find out if you've crossed the line and need to get a life.

Signs That Your Boyfriend Is Your Only Friend

- When you send out an Evite for your birthday, he is the only person who RSVPs.
- You have a "we-mail address." Even worse, that we-mail address is something like iheartmyboyfriend@gmail.com.
- Your only alone time is when you're going to the bathroom (and even then you keep the door open).
- The incoming call log on your cell phone is empty.
- When he goes on a business trip you call your parents to see if they want to hang out. Also, when he's on said business trip, you check in with each other no less than ten times a day.
- You have two friends on MySpace—your boyfriend and Tom.
- When you tell your coworkers that you got engaged their response is "I thought you were already married."
- The last photo taken of you without him in it was two years ago.
- You've taken a vacation to one of those creepy "couples only" resorts in the Caribbean.
- He sits in the room while you get a bikini wax.
- You wish he got a period so you could sync up your cycles.

But, just when you swore you weren't going to ever become *that* girl, the unthinkable happened. You got crazy in love and somehow managed to spend every waking (and nonwaking) moment with *him*. Now that the pheromones have settled and/or your relationship went belly-up, you realize that you had intentionally or inadvertently abandoned the rest of your social circle. You want to make amends with your friends and, at the risk of sounding like a Lifetime "A Moment of Truth Movie," be the woman you once were, but you don't exactly know if they'll welcome you back with open arms.

Well, there's good news, and it's twofold: First of all, with a little effort, you can reconnect with your friends. Second, even though you feel guilty for not being around as much as you should have been, the situation isn't as tragic as you think. Everyone makes mistakes, and love (or what you think at the time is love) sometimes compels people to do things that are out of character, like ditching your astronaut suit and driving across state lines while wearing an adult diaper (or, in your case, going camping with him and pretending that you had absolutely no problemo going numero uno in the flora). Here are some ways to get back in the good graces of your friends and restore some balance and social order to your life.

Step One: Make the First Move

News flash: After you break plans with the girls for the umpteenth time in a row so that you can cheer your boyfriend on as he shreds away at Guitar Hero, you start to get labeled a flake. Your friends don't *hate* you (even though you might feel like they do, which is overdramatic, to say the least), but they have gotten used to the idea of you doing the ditching. Now the ball is in your court. Reach out, make plans, and stick to 'em. Keep in mind, though, that your friends also have lives, so they won't be waiting by the phone to hear from you.

Step Two: Acknowledge Your Absence—and the Elephant in the Room

It's not going to be just like old times—at least not right away. You may feel awkward around your friends, especially when you realize how much you missed out on. *(OMG, when did you get bangs?)* It's also a good idea to say what everyone else is thinking: you're sorry that you had made yourself so scarce. Let them know that you're fully aware of your bad friend behavior and promise to balance out your time going forward. Anybody worth your time should accept your apology and move on.

Step Three: Keep It Up

Don't assume that everything's all good in the hood just because you showed your face at one measly brunch. We all know that actions are stronger than words, so prove to your friends that you meant what you said about changing your ways and actually *being* rather than *talking about being* a good friend. Make the effort. Re-evaluate your priorities. And you could even, gasp, invite your boyfriend along sometimes.

Step Four: Reconnect.

Take a road trip, make weekly lunch dates, have a movie night, set up an *America's Next Top Model* winner's pool—come up with some fun new activities and traditions that will reconnect and keep you connected with your friends. Hell, you could even bust out the Guitar Hero.

Ms Friendship Manners

Dear Miss Friendship Manners,

Question: Hos before bros?

With girl power,
Confused in Kalamazoo

Dear Confused,

Again, with the gutter language. If Ms. Friendship Manners didn't already know that the fine people of Michigan were some of her most well-mannered readers, she would think that there was something in the waters of the northernmost Great Lakes that makes people froth with filth at the mouth.

To answer your question, the idea of always putting the women in your life before the men is a bit strange, considering that we live during a time when men and women are permitted and encouraged to be friends. Life is not a sorority house. Besides, if you have ever been part of a sorority, you know that better confidantes can often be found on the Internet. A more accurate and appealing way to state your case would be to say, "Near and dear friends come before our throwaway romantic interests."

Miss Friendship Manners would like to note that she probably has a few more notches in the bedpost of life than most of her dear readers. With increased age comes increased responsibility. Your friends will always be important to you, but as you grow older, you will need to learn the art of balancing the important people and different facets of your life. It's the polite thing to do.

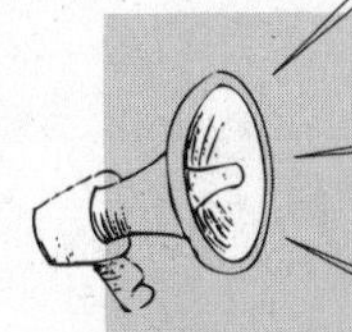

Sounding Off: Time Honored Friend Traditions

Everyone has (or should have) traditions that keep the bonds of friendship strong even when life gets crazy busy. Feel free to steal the following ideas and pass them off as your own.

"My best friend and I watch all the awards shows while stuffing our faces and talking about how horrible and malnourished all the actresses look." —Mary, 28

"The Thursday before Thanksgiving all of my friends come over for a pre-Thanksgiving pot luck. Everyone brings something they would never have with their family, such as lentil loaf, sushi, and peanut butter pie. And of course we have way too much to drink." —Ashley, 27

"Every time one of my college friends gets married we take a picture of the bride peeing while we hold up her dress. It's silly but it makes for a great memory." —JESSICA, 28

"Making cupcakes. Whilst drunk." —LEONORA, 22

"Me and two of my girlfriends get together about once a year for a night of cards. We sit around drinking wine, listening to music, and playing gin rummy. We have so much fun and it gives us time to talk and laugh." —BETHANY, 24

"The girls and I love to get together, order a pizza, and plant our butts on the couch in front of the TV and watch hockey games every weekend." —KRYSTLE, 24

"Every year my friend brings me as her 'date' to her family's Easter brunch at a fancy restaurant, which, for a Jewish girl, is heaven!" —Jen, 31

"My best friend and I go on vacation together every year and we plan to keep the tradition alive once we have kids. Also, a few of my friends watch The Hills *together every week (yes—we're in our mid-to-late twenties). We each drink a bottle of wine and bitch about our lives."* —CHRISTINA, 25

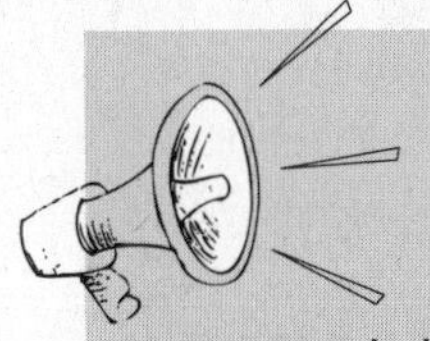

Sounding Off: Breakup Buddy

An overwhelming number of girls we talked to said that they would've never survived a breakup without the help of a good friend. And, surprisingly, the friend they referred to was an actual person, not a bottle of alcohol. Here are their stories:

"The day my boyfriend and I broke up, my friend took the best care of me. First we went for a little retail therapy at Saks Fifth Avenue, where I proceeded to have a tearful breakdown. I was so embarrassed, but she said at least my meltdown was in a very chic place. That night, she took me out for a night on the town. After more than a few cocktails, I was dancing on a banquette, nearly forgetting the breakup. She even made sure I got home safely. I really don't know if I could have gotten through that day without her." —Caroline, 29

"My first big breakup was brutal. It affected me to the point that I couldn't get out of bed in the morning, my grades were dropping, and I was losing weight rapidly. My best friend literally lifted me through the three months when I was a mess. She never got tired of listening to me (and I did quite a lot of talking), even if it was about the same stuff every single day. I credit her with the fact that I'm a lot stronger in my relationships now." —Molly, 22

"After a bad breakup, my friend came with me on a weekend trip to Dublin with no notice at all. We just went online, bought tickets, and left." —SueEllen, 27

"After a horrible breakup my best friend and I took a trip to Buenos Aires and on the first night there we ended up at a nightclub where I met this cute boy. She told me to go for it. He and I made out until she finally gave me the nudge that it was time to leave—at 7 AM*—but the boy begged us to stay out a bit longer. I knew she wanted to go back to the hotel and sleep, since we had been awake for almost twenty-four hours, but she gladly obliged so that I could 'hang out' with him (yes, that's what I feel comfortable calling it, but think of it what you will)."* —SARA, 29

chapter eleven

THREESOMES

(And Get Your Head Out of the Gutter Because We're Not Talking Those Kinds of Threesomes)

Navigating the Sometimes Murky Waters of a Friendship Trio

While we're on the topic of balancing your friends with your significant other, we thought we'd talk about balancing friends with other friends. Don't follow along? Hear us out: According to ancient mysticism (and also according to a Schoolhouse Rock song), three is the magic number. That's because some of the best stuff (wishes, the holy trinity, and the band Nirvana) and some of the worst (the Axis of Evil, celebrity deaths, and the boy band LFO) are all comprised of threes. These trios are only as divine, evil, rocking, or painfully cheesy as the sum of their parts.

However, there's also another type of threesome (and nope, we're still not talking the dirty kind) that's neither all good nor all bad. It's the *ménage à friend,* the friendly trio. When three friends spend a lot of time together, the result can be either dynamic or dramatic. Sure, we're not twelve years old anymore, but groups of three can still cause a bit of drama in adulthood when things go wrong. For instance, how do you deal when you're suddenly stuck in the middle of two feuding friends? Do you play peacekeeper or get in the ring and join the fight? Here, we take a break from our regularly scheduled programming to examine the ups and downs of trios and show you how to ensure that your threesome is awesome.

Thrice as Nice: The Benefits of the Friendly Trio

Andy Warhol once said, "One's company, two's a crowd, and three's a party." Yes, one-plus-one-plus-one can equal security, balance, and fun. For example, take any high school movie. The dweebs come in duos (think *Superbad*'s Seth and Evan). On the other hand, three people make up a bona fide clique (even if it is the Dungeons and Dragons crew). Remember when Napoleon Dynamite teamed up with Deb and Pedro or when Angela Chase started hanging out with Rayanne Graff and Rickie Vasquez in the short-lived masterpiece *My So-Called Life*? Three certainly can be a party.

In addition to earning more social clout as a trio, the dynamics of a group of friends can be preferable to that of a duet. In a functioning threesome, each person adds something unique to the mix and their personalities naturally lend themselves to a common role, like the leader (Cher Horowitz), the pleaser (Donna Martin), or the equalizer (Phoebe Buffay). Life in threes is never really boring.

The Toxic Triangle: Friendship Threesomes Gone Bad

While we're talking a bit about mysticism, let's examine the other side of Zen: when there's light, there must also be dark, and for every happy trio in existence, there are probably triple (pun sort of intended) the number of dysfunctional ones. Some people (and by some people we mean some *men*) speculate that this is due to the inherent insecure and manipulative nature of females, who bond by gossiping about one another. The truth is that it's hard to please more than one person at a time (once again, get your mind out of the gutter), which can make some threesomes prone to jealousy and possessiveness.

Therefore, when things are going well in the threesome, life is good, but when someone in the group isn't happy, it can push the energy balance into negative or even downright uncomfortable territory. The biggest example of this energy shift is when you are caught in the middle of two squabbling friends. Sometimes this is inevitable. How do you handle this situation and emerge with your friendships intact? Well, here are five ways to reestablish peace in threes:

1. In the event of a squabble, refuse to take sides. And, if one of your friends wants to force you to take sides, do the following: Stick your fingers in your ears and yell over and over again, "I'm not listening!"
2. Encourage, rather than facilitate, peace talks between the two warring factions. You want to be supportive, but also as hands-off as possible. If that doesn't work, buy them each a pair of boxing gloves or suggest that

they get themselves to the nearest nightclub and have a dance off to determine the winner of the argument.

3. Try not to speak on behalf of the other party *(Well, I think she feels that . . .)*. Also, never gossip to one friend about the other unless you want to get pulled into the ring.
4. Realize that we aren't in sixth grade anymore. If your friends can't get over their differences, distance yourself from the situation until they figure it out. In the meantime, don't lie if you're hanging out with one friend in order to spare the feelings of the other. This isn't your battle to fight.
5. If they don't respond to your idea about settling their differences via a dance off, suggest it again. Seriously. It sounds like fun.

The Truth About Five Infamous Third Wheels

There was a reason your mother warned you against going to a sleepover party with three friends: because you would inevitably end up with your hand in warm water and your bra in the freezer while Julie and Christine erupted into endless fits of giggles and had a story to tell during homeroom on Monday morning. However, at your ten-year high school reunion, Julie confessed to you (after one too many glasses of house white) that she was already trapped in a loveless marriage and Christine made it all too obvious that she had a bit of an addiction to the painkillers that her doctor liberally prescribed. In every trio, there's the possibility that someone will be the odd man (or woman) out, but sometimes that isn't as bad as you think. Here's a look at a group of infamous third wheels and the good and the bad of their situations.

Spinderella

The bad: It must suck when you're the silent member of an all-girl rap group that's named after the two most popular seasonings. Spinderella should've lobbied to change "Salt-N-Pepa" to "Oregano, Basil, and Garlic Powder."

The bright side: Spinderella might have felt like a third wheel at times, but that didn't stop her from being a hip-hop pioneer. She is and always will be the first truly famous female DJ.

Theodore of the Chipmunks

The bad: His was naïve, shy, and never met a carb he didn't love. (Something no one would let him forget.) Alvin had the charisma, Simon had the brains, and all Theodore had was a green turtleneck dress that clung to his lovely chipmunk lumps. No wonder his name came last in the show's theme song.

The bright side: At least Theodore wasn't responsible for 2007's creepy big screen remake of *Alvin and the Chipmunks*.

Janet Wood

The bad: Janet never stood a chance against Chrissy Snow, the dumb blonde with a preference for skimpy ensembles and side ponytails. A stereotypical brunette, she was loyal and smart (albeit, not the smartest or luckiest in love). Fans of *Three's Company* are still pissed that Janet's wedding was the series finale.

The bright side: Um, Janet was loyal and smart, traits that will hold up long after Chrissy's hair falls flat.

Carnie Wilson

The bad: Carnie's claim to fame was being relegated to the background while her hot sister Wendy and the even hotter Chynna Phillips frolicked half-naked in the group's music videos. Sure, she went on to drop a lot of weight and pose for *Playboy*, but she'll always be the one who Chris Farley parodied (almost too well).

On the bright side: Carnie is the member of the group who has actually had the most staying power. Okay, so part of that "staying power" included a stint on *Celebrity Fit Club*, but that's a much-watch show. Seriously!

Michelle Williams

The bad: Michelle Williams was one third of Destiny's Child before Beyoncé and her gold lamé hot pants got all "Crazy in Love" and Kelly Rowland sang a duet with Nelly expressing his frustration that she had a boo who was also her baby's daddy. Michelle's talents were limited to not vocally overshadowing Beyoncé, not being hotter than Beyoncé, and not being a better dancer than Beyoncé. Poor thing probably believed the queen "B" when she said that the group would get back together after she was finished recording her first solo album.

On the bright side: Michelle went on to have a pretty successful career as a gospel singer. Plus, if you think waaaay back (to, like, the late nineties) Destiny's Child used to be a quartet, so Michelle actually is a survivor because she didn't get her ass kicked out of the group.

It Takes Three:
Activities for You and Your Plus-Two

It doesn't always take two to make a thing go right. Some things can be accomplished only with three (or more) people. Here are some examples:

- Forming an all-girl singing group
- Playing double dutch with a jump rope
- Building a human pyramid
- Scoring a sweet triple room in a college dorm
- Dressing up as Charlie's Angels for Halloween
- Organizing a secret Santa gift swap
- Referring to your friends as your "posse"
- Driving in the diamond/carpool/high-occupancy vehicle lane during rush hour
- Making a conference call (good times, good times)

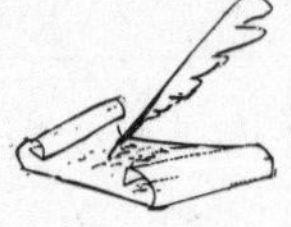

Ms. Friendship Manners

Dear Ms. Friendship Manners,

I know that as women, we've come a long way baby, which is why I'm a bit embarrassed to ask this, but here it goes: for once and for all, what's the proper response when a friend asks you if her pants make her look fat?

With confusion,
Polite in Peoria

Dear Polite,

Honesty is not always the best policy. Ms. Friendship Manners can't believe she just said that. Just a moment, because she needs to take a timeout and breathe into a paper bag until her nerves calm down.

Okay, that's better.

Yes, you should tell the truth most of the time. However, when it comes to certain little things that really make no difference at all but can lead to hurt feelings if you were to open up your yap—for instance, a friend asking for your honest opinion about the size of her derriere in a pair of chinos—keep those lips zipped. If you really can't help yourself, offer constructive noncriticism and steer your friend toward a more flattering outfit choice. Just don't forget to take a long hard look at yourself in the mirror, too.

chapter twelve

WHEN THE FRIENDSHIP SINKS

Breaking Up, Making Up, and Moving On

Breaking up is hard to do. Yeah, yeah, it's not like someone died, but a romantic split is usually followed by the stages of grief: denial *(we'll get back together next week)*; anger *(I gave him everything! I was half a virgin when I met him!)*; bargaining *(I can change. I swear)*; depression *(I'm going to die alone)*; and, finally, acceptance *(I'm better off without him and, besides, he'll be bald in a few years)*. Okay, so maybe there will always be some overflow from the anger stage.

To sum it up, even if you're the one who ended the relationship, breakups can be pretty traumatic: You'll yell, you'll cry, you'll remember the good times and temporarily forget the bad, you'll listen to Morrissey on repeat, and, finally, you'll come to your senses and realize that Gloria Gaynor and a billion drunk karaoke singers can't be wrong: *I will survive*. And you will survive not only because you've got all your life to live and you've got all your love to give, but you also have your circle of friends to help ease your heartache.

There's only one little problem: What happens when a good friend, rather than a boyfriend, gives you the dreaded "It's not you, it's me" speech? Women are supposed to stick together forever and ever, right?

Well, even though it goes against the natural order of things, a friend can most certainly break up with you. In fact, splitting up with a pal might cause you more pain, heartache, and confusion than parting ways with a boyfriend.

Now, you might be thinking: *Well, you've obviously never had your heart ripped out of your chest and punted like a football, because if you knew how bad it hurts to get kicked in the aorta, you'd realize there's no way in H-E-double hockey sticks that losing a friend can be worse than losing a love.*

Point well taken. Yes, nothing can rival that feeling you get in the pit of your stomach when you accidentally-on-purpose glance at the Internet search history on your boyfriend's computer and discover he's been spending a lot of time browsing the "Casual Encounters>men seeking men" section of Craigslist.

Hear us out, though: the problem with friend breakups, besides the fact that they involve *breaking up* with someone, is that no one likes to talk about their BFF giving them the boot (other than emo bands who just love to whine about pain and suffering) or read empowering how-to guides that reassure you that friendships break up only because they're broken, so get back out there, girl, and find someone new who appreciates your fabulous self. The lack of conversation about these types of breakups leads to a lack of social precedent, which means that we have to drive the rocky road from troubled friendship to clean break without the guidance of OnStar or GPS.

In addition to the dearth of friend breakup discussion, here are some other reasons why it's so hard to say good-bye to a friend and, shockingly, why it can even be harder than getting the heave-ho from a guy.

Why Breaking Up with a Friend Can Be More Traumatic Than Breaking Up with a Guy

• **It ain't right:** To reiterate what we just mentioned, there's a reason why we never heard Mr. Rogers sing, "Won't you move out of my neighborhood, because this just isn't working out anymore?" (And it's not because it doesn't rhyme.) We're taught that friends are *supposed* to be forever. They're also supposed to shield us from the storm, pick us up when we're feeling down, and do a bunch of other Hallmark card stuff that makes us feel warm, fuzzy, and loved. (And, to be fair, we should do the same for them.) In reality, life is not a Hallmark card and sometimes really bad things happen that drive otherwise good people apart.

• **You miss the ending:** As women, we're conditioned to avoid confrontation, unless it's the unhealthy, weave-pulling, male-fantasy fulfilling, reality-show variety. Therefore, we have no idea how to deal with losing a friend. Often, friendship breakups offer no closure: no tearful phone calls, no Dear John letters, no ceremonial return of a cardboard box containing the things that you borrowed from her a long time ago, such as CDs, that cute pair of strappy red sandals, and a dog-eared copy of Pamela Anderson's best-selling novel, *Star*. (Don't be a hater. It's a great beach read.)

All too often, when we break up with a friend, we fade to black rather than coming to a logical conclusion. This tragic nonending leaves the dumped party wondering what she did wrong or—even worse—completely unaware that the friendship is over. Like that poor, overgrown puppy who peed on the floor one too many times and got dropped off at the pound but still waits patiently in a cage for his owner to come back for him, the dumpee will never know that she's been abandoned. Actually, that visual just made us cry a little bit. Sorry about that.

- **You'll have to go it alone:** So you actually believe that the other members of your posse will drop by your apartment bearing cupcakes, trashy magazines, and a bottle of vodka to help you ease the pain of a friend breakup? Well, think again, Hester Prynne. Unlike the time when your boyfriend traded you in for a newer model and your closest confidantes offered moral support and told you exactly what you wanted to hear (*you're great; he sucks*), those same friends will steer clear of this particular train wreck.

This is because no one—we repeat, no one—wants to get caught between two feuding friends. (Plus, those "Team Aniston/Angelina" shirts are sooooo 2005.) Can you really blame them? Emotions are running high and it's a lose-lose situation for everyone involved. You're on your own, kid.

- **A lifelong mourning period:** Many of us believe that when you break up with someone, the following formula applies:

> the length of the relationship in months / 2 = the amount of time, in months, it will take for your heart to go on

This is all well and good if you spent a few months with Johnny Ex, but what happens when you and your friend have a long history together that goes back to a time when you wet your bed and not because you drank too many gin-and-tonics (and that only happened *one* time, all right)?

Also, after a friend breakup, you'll never regain the sense of hope that comes with romance, the possibility that a dark, handsome, yet quirkily endearing Paul Rudd look-alike could waltz up to you tomorrow in the organic section of the supermarket and make you forget about the former love of your life. The truth is that all of the new friends in the world can't replace the one who broke your heart.

- **And, finally, the classic breakup line "let's stay friends" obviously doesn't apply in this situation.**

This pretty much speaks for itself.

Why Do Friendships Sink?

Now we've explored why friend breakups hurt so badly, but why do they happen in the first place? Here are three theories:

1. Umm . . . because she hates you.
2. Did we mention that she hates you?
3. Knock. Knock.
   Who's there?
   She hates.
   She hates WHO?
   She hates you.

Just kidding! Well, actually, we're only sort of kidding. Friend breakups happen for many different reasons, ranging from a huge blowout to a gentle drift when two people grow up and apart from each other. Here's a closer look at the most common reasons for a friendship split:

Someone Commits An Unforgivable Offense

To err is human, and, luckily, many friends are divine and can forgive a lapse in judgment. Of course, no one is a saint, so the likelihood of forgiveness depends on the severity of the "oops." For example, "Oops, I didn't realize I was having sex with your boyfriend" or "Oops, I didn't think you'd mind that I opened up three credit card accounts in your name and then charged $10,000 in really expensive makeup, shoes, and handbags" usually falls under the "I never want to see your skank face again" category. However, transgressions such as "Oops, I kissed a guy you went out on one date with three years ago" or "Oops, I spilled wine on that dress I borrowed from you" shouldn't cause any earth-shattering drama.

It's unfortunate, but sometimes someone you thought was a friend commits an act so heinous that "sorry" won't make everything better. As a result, a breakup ensues or you take the bitch to *The People's Court* and let Judge Milian rip her a new one.

You Gently Drift Apart

It's a sad fact of life: People change, and sometimes they grow apart. In the case of the gentle drift, nothing in particular signals the end of your friendship. Instead, as the list of things you have in common gets shorter and shorter, your friendly bond unravels, leaving only indifference and a quickly waning sense of obligation behind. You call each other out of habit rather than genuine interest and learn what's going on in your respective lives via mutual friends. Basically, you're just going through the motions.

Then, after months pass by and you can't remember the last time you talked to her, you finally stop denying the obvious: you've both moved on.

The gentle drift results in a quite mature and civil *non*-breakup. There's no mudslinging, no smear campaign, no anonymous phone call to her boyfriend about what *really* happened in

Vegas. However, just because you're not bitter doesn't mean your feelings are totally neutral. You still have happy memories that make you long for the way things used to be. Before you start reminiscing about your friendship, realize that the past is in the past and there's no going back—at least until Mac develops a time-traveling iPod. And in the meantime, if you ever get the urge to find out if her life is going better than yours, just stalk her on Google, MySpace, and Facebook.

You Thought It Was a Good Idea to Live (or Backpack Through Europe) Together

Every freshman dorm has them: the attached-at-the-hip best friends from high school who both applied (early admissions) so they could room together in the coolest building and stretch the best years of their lives into the next four years (or five or six, depending on how many times they switch majors).

Of course, we all know how this story goes. After the novelty of living away from their parents wears off, so does the novelty of sharing a tiny living space and an even tinier fridge. Their bad habits start to drive each other nuts, and after one too many squabbles about the cable bill, the friends who were once so inseparable that they were nicknamed the Olsen twins seek refuge away from each other. One half of the duo discovers psychedelic drugs and slam poetry, while the other pledges a sorority. And before you can say "transfer," these former BFF's figure out a way to give each other the silent treatment for the remainder of the year, even though they share a ten-by-ten-foot living space.

These types of breakups don't only happen with roommates. They can also take place whenever two people are forced to spend lots of time together, like on vacation in a faraway land. You're good friends, so you'll have a good time traipsing through Europe together for the summer, right? Um, not necessarily.

Sure, it seems logical to live or vacation with your very best friend, but cohabitation and travel can bring out the worst—or, at the very least, the weirdest—behavior in people. Plus, it's harder to argue with a friend over things like rent or money without it negatively impacting your relationship.

Before you sign the lease on that apartment or book those plane tickets, you might want to test the waters with a few sleepovers or weekend trips together. Be honest with each other so you don't have to find out the hard way that she's a total toilet paper Nazi who also likes to clip her toenails in the kitchen or that her idea of roughing it involves staying at three-star rather than four-star hotels.

Now this isn't to say that close friends can't be roommates or travel buddies. It just all comes down to compatibility, tolerance levels, and your ability to deal in confined spaces and stressful situations. If you're still worried about your travel/roommate compatibility with a close confidante, choose to live and/or travel with someone you like well enough as a friend, but don't love like a sister.

The Friendship Is Toxic

You two go together like Sid and Nancy, children and matches, or stripes and plaids. You're just a bad combination, a toxic twosome. Perhaps you always knew that the friendship was flawed but didn't know how to handle it, or maybe you never realized that the way she treated you wasn't so friendly after all (see Chapter Six: "Frenemies: The Users, Losers, and Abusers Who

You Need to De-MySpace Right Now" on page 91). Then again, there's also the possibility that *you're* the problem in the relationship. In that case, you probably need to go back to school—in particular, kindergarten—and learn how to treat others kindly.

No matter how you discover that you're no good for each other, it's best to spare the long painful ordeal and give this broken friendship the needle and some much-needed relief from a negative force in your life. (See "The Breakup Helper" on page 200.)

There's a Personal Crisis

We know it's hard to believe, but not everything is about you. Sometimes a friend drops off the face of the earth because she's going through some particularly hard times and has bigger worries than what bar to hit up on a Saturday night.

Sure, it's your duty to ask a friend in need if there's anything you can do to help her out, but if her answer is "no," respect her space. We know this is also hard to believe, but some people prefer to deal with issues on their own, rather than blabbering on and on about their personal business over mimosas and egg white omelets at a crowded brunch spot.

A friend in pain may even cut out all communication with you until she feels strong enough to resume her normal life and relationships. Try to be understanding and, again, don't take it personally.

Also, it's a common misconception that friendship has to be all or nothing at all, in or out, absent or present. Sometimes people get preoccupied with the craziness that is life. It doesn't mean that she hates you.

You Think You Know . . . But You Have No Idea

Perhaps the most common reason for a friend breakup is the nonreason. Much like crop circles, Bigfoot, and the Bermuda Triangle, the reason your friendship sank will remain completely and utterly mysterious.

The Breakup Helper

Just like there are many reasons for a friendship to end, there are a number of ways in which the breakup can go down. The best way to deal with a breakup is directly, but not so directly that your fist ends up in her face. Types of breakups include: the big bang (the friendship blows up); the cold turkey (you completely cut her off, like ripping off a Band-Aid in one quick motion); the phase out (slowly remove her from your life); and the downgrade (you reduce the friendship from platinum, near-and-dear confidante to gold-plated acquaintance).

Surefire Breakup Tips for the Dumper (Hehe, We Said "Dumper")

When it comes to romantic relationships, there's this mutual understanding that things might not work out. This doesn't apply to friendship, which is why it's so difficult to give someone the pink slip without feeling like you're doing something unbelievably evil. But with a lot of sympathy and some solid tips (listed on the following pages), you can lessen some of the blow by ending it in the most distinguished way possible. Here's how to ditch without looking like a total bitch:

- **You'd better think.** Dumping a friend isn't like dyeing your hair or becoming a vegan. Once you go through with it, there's no turning back, since it's doubtful that she'll be overjoyed if you change your mind. Before you do something that will hurt another person, make sure that you're not just pissed off about something silly that can't be resolved with a little bit of time apart from each other.
- **Don't leave her hanging on like a yo-yo.** If you make the decision to let a friend go, the least you can do is offer her an explanation. Remember to treat her like you would want to be treated and be as honest as possible while also trying to minimize the heartache. Choose a neutral meeting place where you can comfortably share your feelings with her, but not a place that's as comfortable as, say, your favorite Mexican joint, Wacky El Cantina, home of the Monster Megarita. You want to go into the conversation with a clear (aka sober) head. And if you can't bear the thought of looking her in the face over a plate of cheesy biscuits at Red Lobster, write your thoughts down and give her a letter. Here's a helpful tip, though: skip the e-mail unless you want the entire e-universe to know what went down between the two of you.
- **Prepare for tears.** As we mentioned above, after you tell her that you want to end things, she's not going to curtsy, say "Thank you," then disappear from your life forever. There will be tears. Lots of them. She may even say some very unpleasant things to you, then about you on her blog, her MySpace page, her Facebook page, and maybe even her away message on IM. As much as it sucks, put yourself in her shoes. You'd feel just as hurt, angry, and betrayed as she does.

- **Make like Ron Burgundy and stay classy.** All of that being said, if you happen to run into her, be prepared to do the bob and weave, especially if the first post-breakup encounter happens at a bar. Fueled by a potent blend of blind rage and liquid courage, your ex might want to air her grievances in a public forum. Whatever she says, take the high road and resist the urge to yell and scream back like a crazy methhead on *Cops*. That won't do anything except keep onlookers totally riveted.
- **You'll be found guilty.** After parting ways with a pal, it's only natural that you'll experience feelings of guilt. You might ask yourself questions like, What could I have done differently? Am I a horrible person? Or, Where can I buy a whip so I can flagellate away my sins? To put it simply, don't be surprised if you have a burning desire to put on your best *woe is me* outfit (which most likely includes a pair of pajama pants) and throw a big old self-pity party.

Now, before you go all medieval martyr, hear us out. Guilt is a lot like stress in that it's helpful and effective—sometimes. Think about it: On one hand, there's *eustress*, a good form of anxiety that often accompanies the big things in life, like a major promotion at work or buying your first home. At the opposite end of the spectrum, we have *distress*, the negative (and more common) prolonged type of tension that can push a normally cool, calm, and collected person into bitchy, twitchy, and frazzled territory.

When taken in the correct dosage, guilt can be very useful. It lets us know when we should right a wrong, make amends, and take steps to correct our not-so-nice behavior. One could say that to err is human, but feeling guilty can help make us into better people. However, as women, we often suffer from guilt overload and me-last syndrome. But should this really come as a surprise? There are countless industries that thrive by manufacturing guilt and then selling antidotes in the form of women's magazines, anti-cellulite cream, and fat-free potato chips that taste exactly like the real thing but may lead to oily anal discharge.

Yes, breaking up with a friend isn't easy, but don't forget about the reasons why you bid her adieu in the first place, the most important being that she really hasn't been a friend to you. A frenemy, a toxic pal, an enabler, a drama queen—whatever you want to call her—is a destructive force. To paraphrase what Mary J. Blige sang in "No More Drama" and, come to think about it, just about every song except "Real Love" and "Family Affair": "No more, no more drama!!!!!! No more! No more! No more!!!" Once you realize that you've flushed some toxins from your system, you'll redirect the guilt, learn how to be more positive, and focus some much-needed attention on the good people in your life. You've made the decision to let her go, so now you need to let it go. And remember to eat those Olestra chips in moderation.

On the Flip Side, If You've Been Dumped . . .

Obviously, the best thing you can do when a friend breaks up with you is cling to her leg and sob, "Whhhhyyyyyyy?" Sorry, that's the best thing you can do if you want to lose your last shred of dignity. It is possible to make it through the devastation with your self-esteem intact and even grow from the experience. Here's how:

- **Take it personally, but realize that it might not be personal.** Unless your friend has already alienated her entire social circle and you were the last woman standing by her side, it's only normal that you ask yourself, "What's wrong with me?" when a friend cuts you loose. But, as we mentioned earlier, the question might really be "what's wrong with her?" since she might be going through something and needs to detach herself from the friendship while she's working it out. Before you make incorrect assumptions and go down the wrong road, figure out what's really behind the breakup.
- **Do the right thing.** If you've come to the conclusion that you're the reason the friendship has hit its expiration date, then make like M.J. and take a long look at the man in the mirror. Are you the person you want to be? Do you treat your friends the way you want them to treat you? If the answer is no, you should apologize to the party you have offended and take responsibility. It might not change things, but it's an important step on your road to recovery from total douchey-ness.
- **Have some "me time."** Even if you were the one to blame for the breakup, you're still allowed to retreat from the social scene for a bit to lick your wounds. Rather than wallowing in self-pity, do something positive that will help you become a better friend in the future. You could move to an ashram and embark on a spiritual journey through meditation, yoga, and therapeutic arts and crafts, or you could just learn from your mistakes and not screw things up again.

Reunited and It Feels So Good: How an Ex Can Come Back in Your Life

The saying "time heals all wounds" should really be more like "time heals *some* wounds." Some friendships might never be mendable, but for others reconciliation might be possible after you've both had an opportunity to gain some perspective on things. For example, let's say your friend asked your honest opinion of her new boyfriend and you honestly told her that he sucked, an off-handed comment that opened up a Pandora's box of pent-up bad stuff. She accused you of being jealous, you called her insecure, things get ugly, and before you know it, the friendship is over. That is, until several months later when she realizes that you were right—her boyfriend really is a total tool. She reaches out to you and within minutes you're both crying tears of joy and vowing to never fight again.

The odds of a reunion are even better if one of you has a big event like marriage, pregnancy, divorce, or death, and in a reflective moment, decides that life is too short to stay angry, especially over something petty.

And of all your former friends, it is probably the one you grew apart from or lost touch with who has the best odds for a second chance. When a friendship runs out of batteries without any drama, it can be jump-started again when both parties remember why they liked each other so much in the first place and vow to make more of an effort this time around.

Famous Friend Breakups

Perhaps the only friend breakups that hurt more that our own are the ones that happen between people we don't know or, better yet, people who don't exist in real life. These are the feuds that had us wailing and hollering, "Why God, whyyyyyyyy?!"

Paris Hilton and Nicole Richie

Thanks to their undeniable talent and years of hard work, these childhood friends pulled themselves up by the bootstraps, got off the streets, and quickly became Hollywood's hottest BFFs—until their friendship mysteriously collapsed in early 2005. The only explanation for their break was Paris's cryptic assertion, "[Nicole] knows what she did." The world lit candles, held hands, and prayed that these two role models would reunite. In October 2006, our prayers were answered when Paris and Nicole ended their feud and reconciled.

Brenda Walsh and Kelly Taylor

While Brenda spent her summer pretending to be French, chain-smoking, and eating cow brains in Paris, her best friend Kelly started up an illicit affair with Brenda's boyfriend, Dylan. After learning about the affair, a betrayed Brenda told Kelly and Dylan, "I hate you both. Never talk to me again." Brenda eventually forgave them, because otherwise, things would've been a bit awkward at the Peach Pit for the next few seasons until Brenda hightailed it to London for good.

Rosie O'Donnell and Elisabeth Hasselbeck

Question: What do you get when you mix a liberal lesbian

with a conservative Christian? Answer: The only episode of *The View* worth watching. Prior to Rosie and Elisabeth's showdown, the two claimed to be friends, albeit unlikely ones. However, after several days of bickering about the war in Iraq, the shit hit the fan and the producers for the morning gabfest went to split screen to showcase the two cohosts exchanging heated words. On a video blog Rosie posted on her Web site following their blow-up, she said that she had never tried harder to be friends with someone, but doesn't think she succeeded with Elisabeth. Elisabeth's response: "I did define us as friends, but I'm not going to make the leap to assume that we will or will not be friends in the future."

Lauren "LC" Conrad and Heidi Montag

It was all sushi, fro-yo and "hos before bros" for these two roommates throughout the first season of *The Hills*. Then Spencer Pratt came along during season two and ripped apart one of reality television's tightest twosomes. LC tried to warn Heidi that Spencer was a manipulative cheater, but Heidi wasn't hearing it and she decided to move in with Spencer, leaving LC in the dust. The final blow came when LC accused the conniving couple of starting a rumor that she had a sex tape with her ex Jason, who is worthy of a whole book. Luckily, the cameras were rolling when LC confronted Heidi in one of the best made-for-TV bitch fights of all time. The only thing that would make this breakup worse is if it were actually real, rather than scripted.

Cady Heron and Regina George

Cady Heron didn't know what she was getting into when she befriended Regina George and her "army of skanks." This became apparent when Cady admitted that she had a crush on

Regina's ex. Regina offered to help get them together by shoving her tongue down his throat. Cady then sought revenge by sabotaging Regina's social standing. Of course, Cady's vengeful plan ended up turning her into her own worst enemy—and a total bitch. But, in the end, everyone learned a valuable lesson: Lindsay Lohan looks best as a redhead.

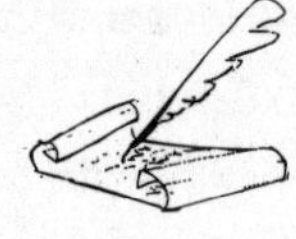

Ms. Friendship Manners

Dear Ms. Friendship Manners,

I have a friend who is quite frugal. Scratch that—she's cheap. Every time we go out to dinner, I dread the moment when the check arrives and I have to pretend to act surprised that she forgot her wallet or is running low on cash. How do I politely tell her that she owes more than $8 for her salad, glass of wine, and portobello mushroom burger?

Heaps of thank-yous with a cherry on top,
Broke and Hungry in Brooklyn

Dear Broke and Hungry,

All of this talk about food is making Ms. Friendship Manners's tummy rumble. Did you hear it? Please excuse her.

Unfortunately, the almighty dollar has destroyed

many a good friendship. For this reason alone, you should make sure that you get your facts straight before you shake down your skinny-walleted pal for some extra cash. Are you splitting your checks fairly? For example, what if she usually opts for only a side salad and tap water, while you prefer to attack the filet mignon or Maine lobster with the veracity of a feral beast? Making your dining companion chip in for your expensive tastes is quite the opposite of proper.

Also, you want to consider your friend's financial situation. Is she struggling to get through grad school while you toil away in a gilded office as a corporate lawyer? If you come from opposite sides of the financial spectrum, you may want to choose cheaper dining options or, better yet, offer to treat your financially disadvantaged friend to the good life every once in a while.

However, if she is more than capable of paying her way, there are a few ways to deal with a miser: You can kindly ask your waiter for separate checks. If you can't get separate checks, you can use your wonderful math skills and let your friend know exactly what she owes, although, in Ms. Friendship Manners's humble opinion, it's not worth making a federal case over a dollar or two. Be discreet and courteous, rather than loudly proclaiming for the entire dining room to hear, "Gimme my money, woman!"

If none of these things work and you want to stay friends with this person, Miss Manners suggests skipping dinner and meeting her for coffee instead or skipping coffee and inviting her to your apartment, where you can sit and stare at each other. That doesn't cost a dime.

chapter thirteen

MISERY LOVES COMPANY

The Challenges of Making New Friends

We've already talked about the fact that we get by with a little help from our friends and that breaking up is hard to do. Now, what happens when you need some new friends in your life? Whether you've moved across the country and are so desperate for human contact that you call up the cable company just to say hi or you want to broaden your horizons and add some fresh faces to your already-existing social circle, sometimes you need to make connections with new people. Unfortunately, finding compatible confidantes can be more challenging than following the story line on *Lost*.

Yep, it's another dirty little secret about friendship: Making new friends (and real, authentic twenty-four-karat ones, as opposed to casual acquaintances) when you're a certified grown-up sure as hell ain't easy. Plus, the degree of difficulty only goes up as we get up there in years.

Here's the thing: once you graduate from formal education, you also leave behind the controlled social environment it provides. Sure, the real world offers plenty of activities, classes, and clubs where you can meet new people, but you actually have to put in the effort and seek these opportunities out. This all sounds doable enough, until you realize that we live in an increasingly convenient world, where "nesting," ordering in groceries and movies, and worshipping at the altar of the almighty TiVo seems more desirable than getting out there and, you know, getting a life.

Another reason why making friends isn't as easy as the good old days of play dates and elementary school is because people are doing their own thing now (and so are you). Sometimes it seems like everyone else has this fulfilling life—an impenetrable mix of family, friends, work, and social obligations—and no room whatsoever on their calendars for newcomers. Or perhaps you're entering that phase in your twenties also known as the "bridal wave," a flurry of white and taffeta when it feels like all of your friends are marrying off and leaving you behind for a life filled with domestic bliss and nice little Saturday afternoons spent at Bed, Bath & Beyond.

Fear not, though, because many of your fears about friendship are actually unfounded. For example, that woman with the seemingly full dance card probably would love to meet new people, and just because a friend gets married doesn't mean that she stops being your friend. Maybe we need to let our guard down and trust people a little more (but not so much that we send $1,000 to the Nigerian "prince" who e-mailed us last week promising a share of his multimillion-dollar fortune as soon as he can free it from a foreign bank account).

We also shouldn't forget one of the cardinal rules of making new friends: you get what you give. But, before you can even give anything, you gotta' get off the couch and get out there.

Making Friends: An Introspective Retrospective

The qualities we look for in a friend change as we grow older and wiser. They have to; otherwise, we'd still be picking our confidantes based on how many Barbie dolls they own. In adulthood, we become less superficial. We also get to know ourselves better, which, in turn, allows us to befriend those who share similar values, morals, and interests. Let's take a look back at how we formed our social circle over the years and look forward to how we're going to make new friends in the future.

Infancy to Early Childhood

According to the experts, children don't start choosing their own friends until their third birthdays. So, before you blow out three candles on the cake and realize that crapping in your shorts is something to be ashamed of, your family takes charge of making friends for you. Once a week, you and your besties all drool and cry in one another's presence while your moms debate the benefits of breast-feeding. Inevitably, there will be an embarrassing moment some years down the road (usually during your teenage years) when your mother introduces you to Brian, the boy from your first playgroup—"You know, the one who's in the bathtub with you in that picture."

Elementary School

Once you start riding that big yellow bus (or the short bus—yes, some of us will be a little slower to develop than others), you also start taking charge of your social destiny. Nevertheless, proximity and your parents' rules help mold your social circle. Since you're not allowed to ride your bike outside of a four-block radius, you mainly hang out with the neighborhood gang. Of course, you also find yourself drawn to status symbols, quickly befriending the kids who are spoiled with the newest Nintendo games, pantries stocked with sugary cereals and Cheetos, and unlimited access to MTV and HBO. Ah, the joys of absentee parenting.

Middle School

Welcome to the really, really awkward years. During middle school, insecurity flows out of your oversized pores and you wonder if you'll be stuck in a training bra and braces forever. And, like every confused and underdeveloped pre-teen, you do whatever it takes to fit in with the cool crowd, even if it means ditching all your old friends for the girls who have perfectly shiny hair and first names that end in *i* or *y*. (They will also peak during high school, but you won't realize any of this until your ten-year reunion). Sure, your new "friends" often prank call you from slumber parties that you weren't invited to or conveniently forget to save you a seat at the lunch table, but at least being spotted with them at the mall makes you semi-cool by association.

High School

Whether you are a brain, mean girl, jockess, or a band geek, you most likely belong to a clique in high school. The upside of social self-segregation is that you and your friends all share the same interests; the downside is that, well, you and your friends all share the same interests. For the most part, you steer clear of the general student population and are happy to exist in your teenage bubble—that is, until a house party on graduation night when Ethan Embry professes his love for you in a letter that you almost didn't read because you throw it away to signify your disgust with all men.

College

During the first semester of college, making friends works pretty much the same way it did when you were eight years old. Once again, proximity shapes your social life and you quickly form bonds with your roommate and people who live on the same floor as you do. Also, the contained social environment of a college campus acts as a great equalizer. Since everyone lives in tiny dorm rooms and sleeps in bunk beds, you can easily forget that you are on full scholarship and struggling to pay for your education, while your new best friend is an heiress to a multigazillion-dollar vacuum cleaner empire and will never have to work a day in her life.

The early months of college are a flurry of activity, and every Thursday, Friday, and Saturday night, you and ten of your brand-new nearest and dearest head to house parties together, arms linked and minds open, ready to drink cheap swill out of big red keg cups and make new memories (or nights that you don't remember but later look back at photos and assume that they were fun). This open-minded attitude is nice and all, but as your college career progresses beyond 101 classes, you add and subtract friends to your circle until you find a group that clicks and becomes your very own version of a framily.

Your Twenties

While there's a small grace period right after college when everyone desperately tries to hold on to the undergraduate lifestyle (that is, drinking on weeknights and eating pizza for breakfast) and the last vestiges of their youth, reality eventually sets in and you realize that those years are best left behind you. Things aren't better or worse, just different.

There's still plenty of fun to be had, but things aren't what they used to be. Case in point: You start collecting people from all facets and phases of your life, so by the time you reach your mid-twenties, your friends seem more like a la carte items on a menu than a prix-fixe meal. Also around this time you start befriending people outside of your age range and you realize that—shockingly enough—your parents are people too.

Your day-planner overflows with commitments, you have at least three new voice-mail messages at all times, and you never have to go to the movies alone. These are good times indeed—that is, until the quarter-life crisis hits and your friends all scatter in different directions, kind of like the roaches do when you come home after a long, depressing day at work and turn on the lights in your equally depressing studio apartment, and how pathetic is it that you live, eat, and sleep in the same room? What are you doing with your life? Oh—did we forget to mention that you are going through your own quarter-life crisis?

All of the sudden, your tight-knit framily is spread all over the place (thank goodness for e-mail) and, for the first time in a while, you're without plans on a Friday night. You want to make some new friends, but you have absolutely no idea where or how to find them. Just don't mention any of this to your mom or she'll try to put you in touch with your old playgroup pals. (You know, we hear that Brian is single, and he has a very good job. . . .)

Beyond the Quarter-Life Crisis

They say that your thirties are way better than your twenties. We're assuming that "they" are the thirty-somethings featured in those "in my sexual prime," "top of my career," "love being a mom" articles in women's magazines. The reality is that these years are marked with just as much uncertainty as ever. Seemingly perfect marriages crumble, happy couples feel pressured to procreate, and your parents are getting older, which makes you think a lot more about mortality. Luckily, you've developed the confidence and self-reliance that you wish you had back when you were young and foolish, and you've also become a better judge of character. As a result, your friendships are stronger, deeper, and more fulfilling than ever.

Way, Waaaaaay Beyond the Quarter-Life Crisis (aka Your Golden Girls Years)

You'll be friends with anyone around your age who is still alive.

Eleven Ways You Can Expand Your Social Circle (and That Don't Require That You Convert to Scientology)

We know we said earlier that the older you get the harder it is to make friends, but that doesn't mean it can't be done. There isn't a set formula for how to go about it and some of our suggestions may seem as appealing as watching paint dry, but there is one thing that is nonnegotiable—you must extricate your butt from the couch. New friends aren't going to come knocking on your door, unless, of course, you want to befriend a vacuum cleaner salesman, the Domino's delivery guy, or your friendly neighborhood religious zealot who only wants to take a few minutes of your time to talk about the apocalypse and whether or not you have been "saved." So stop feeling sorry for yourself, get out of your apartment, and go where there's real, live people, as opposed to ones in HDTV. That was step one. Here's what you can do next.

1. **Volunteer.** Not only does it feel good to do some good, but you'll potentially meet an interesting array of people, ranging from a fellow kind soul with a heart of gold to a convicted felon with a thousand hours of community service.
2. **Fake it until you make it.** Are you more of a shy caterpillar than a social butterfly? No worries, because you, too, can learn how to come out of your cocoon a bit. You don't have to become someone that you're not (like a crazy party girl), but you will have to put yourself out there in order to get something in return. There's

no getting around it, you're going to have to perfect the fine art of conversation if you want to make new friends. If you're up for it, practice exchanging niceties with strangers everywhere you can—at the grocery store, the dry cleaner, and your favorite place to grab a hot cup of java. A simple "hi," "lovely weather we're having," or "thank you" are all good small-talk stepping stones. Still feeling uncomfortable? Then, make like a bored wife stuck in a loveless marriage and fake it. If you pretend to be more confident in social situations, you'll eventually trick yourself into actually becoming more confident.

3. **Get busy.** A rolling stone gathers no moss, so go enroll yourself in a class or an activity that interests you. Chances are that you'll meet some likeminded people. Pick your poison: join a knitting circle, play the guitar, learn how to brew your own beer, or play on a coed soccer team. It doesn't really matter what you do, as long as you have fun doing it.
4. **Fall into a routine.** Not only is there comfort in the familiar, but there's also potential to make new friends. Make your world a smaller place by becoming a "regular." Search out a new favorite café or restaurant and hit it up on a frequent basis. You're bound to see the same faces, strike up conversation, and get some free food out of the deal.
5. **Use virtual reality to make real-life connections.** Anyone who has ever taken a stab at online dating knows that people don't always accurately represent themselves in cyberspace. Let us translate: "tall, dark, hand-

some, and professional" often means "short, emotionally stunted, and still living with his mother." Despite this drawback, social networking sites make it easy to get back in touch with old friends in addition to meeting new ones. The trick is to transition your virtual friendships into living and breathing ones by seeking out classes, sports, and activities in your area. If you're part of an online community, you can also attend or organize a real-life gathering with other members near you. Trust your instincts, though. If your "online buddy" wants to meet up in a secluded spot and demands that you come alone, you should totally go . . . if you want to end up on the evening news and then the basis for an episode of *CSI*.

6. **Use your existing friends.** Sometimes the best resource for meeting new people is right in front of you: your existing friends. Meeting friends of friends is a lot like getting set up on a date, minus the boy-girl worries that come with a possible romantic attraction, since she's not judging you based on your cleavage. You already know that your "date" has good references, plus the fact that she's going out with you means that she's also in the market for a new friend.
7. **Manage your expectations.** We don't usually (okay, never) follow *The Rules,* when it comes to dating, but when it comes to making friends, those bitches may have been on to something when they warned against making yourself too available. Bombarding a potential pal with phone calls, text messages, and e-mails might say "thoughtful" to you, but most likely it shouts "des-

perate." Keep in mind that not every person you meet is going to become your next BFF, a real friendship can't be forced, and dressing exactly like her isn't a compliment—it's a sign of instability.

8. **Mix work and play.** You're probably thinking: *You mean hang out with the people that I already spend the majority of my day with in a setting that is the closest thing to a contained environment like school? How genius!* Okay, so it's not the most mind-blowing suggestion, but maybe you haven't given your coworkers a fair shot. Just because you don't share their enthusiasm for Rachael Ray's psychotic perkiness doesn't mean you can't hang out with them socially once in awhile. Plus, we're sure that there is at least one person in your office who is as delightfully twisted as you are. Your challenge is to find her (or him).
9. **Go it alone.** Guys always say that they're more likely to approach a girl who is hanging out by herself because she seems less intimidating than one who is surrounded by a pack of friends. The same rule applies when it comes to making friends. How is anyone supposed to know that you're open to meeting new people if you're always playing croquet and eating corn nuts with the Heathers?
10. **Get a dog.** We'd never advocate substituting human companionship for that of a canine, but what we *do* recommend is using your pet (specifically a dog, which brings out the friendly in everyone unless they have a dark festering hole where their heart should be) as a way to meet friends. After a few trips to the dog park you can arrange playdates for your pooch and use

them as an opportunity to get to know the other dog owners better. Also, animals are built in conversation topics, so your four-legged friend will give people who would otherwise never talk to you a reason to stop and chat. Just make sure you get a really cute dog with a good disposition. No one wants to pet one of those creepy hairless Chinese Cresteds.

11. **Accept each and every invitation that comes your way.** Yes, there are some exceptions to this rule. You have our permission to politely decline any invite that seems like a pyramid scheme, a cult, or an attempt to trick you into being the designated driver. While we're at it, feel free to say "thanks, but no thanks" to sex toy, Tupperware, and kitchen gadget parties. Sometimes it really is better to stay home by yourself and watch *She's the Man*.

How *Not* to Make Small Talk

Now that you know where to find new friends you're probably wondering how to approach them. Well, we can't really put words in your mouth beyond "hi," but we can tell you how to clear a room quicker than a Slayer song.

- Will you be my surrogate?
- Sometimes I just look in the mirror and say to myself, "Gosh, I make a lot of money."
- Have you ever had that not-so-fresh feeling?

- You look just like my twin sister. It's a shame what happened to her.
- It's like my therapist always says . . .
- What's the big deal about the death penalty, anyway?
- I'll steal anything that isn't tied down. Isn't that a scream?
- Well, at least the burning sensation seems to be going away. Now, if I could just do something about the itching . . .
- You wear your weight well.
- Every summer I like to go off my meds just for fun.
- Pretending that I'm pregnant always works for me.
- I think I'm in love with you.

chapter fourteen

EVERYTHING YOU NEED TO KNOW ABOUT FRIENDSHIP YOU LEARNED IN KINDERGARTEN—RIGHT?

We've talked about high school quite a bit in this book, so let's go back even further, to the basics. Take a look at the following elementary school mantras and see how they hold up against the reality of grown-up friendships, where things aren't always as black and white as chalk on the board in the front of the classroom.

THE RULE: Sharing is caring.

THE REALITY: Despite what your art teacher taught you in second grade, you don't have to let your friends in on everything. Sure, it's nice to share stuff like memories, laughs, dessert, clothes, good times and bad times, your hopes and fears, blah blah blah. However, there is that fine line between being generous and overstepping your boundaries. Things better left unshared include your true feelings about her idiotic boyfriend, "interesting" new haircut, or dream of becoming the next American Idol. Also best kept to yourself: unsolicited "advice" about her love life, caloric intake, and career choice. Put yourself in her shoes. You go to your friends for support—not unconstructive criticism. That's what mothers are for.

THE RULE: Keep your hands to yourself.

THE REALITY: Unless you're dressing up with a friend as Krystle Carrington and Alexis Carrington Colby for Halloween or sparring in your cardio kickboxing class, there's never a legitimate reason for hair pulling, pushing, slapping, or any kind of physical contact that would make a guy yell, "Rip her shirt off!" The only potential good that can come out of a catfight is Internet fame. Besides, it's much classier to take the high road and scrawl her digits on the wall of a bathroom stall.

THE RULE: Use your words.

THE REALITY: Back in the day (aka the eighties), Danny Tanner was able to resolve every major girl issue with a good old heart-to-heart talk (and a group hug). If only it were that easy in reality. Most of us would rather avoid confrontation at all costs, preferring to marinate in our own anger instead of risking a fight with a friend. But what you're really doing is initiating a passive-aggressive game of mind reader—waiting for the person who upset you to figure it out on their own and ask *you* what's wrong. So the next time a friend hurts your feelings, think WWDTD (What would Danny Tanner do?). That's right, talk to her—preferably within a thirty-minute time frame (including commercial breaks).

THE RULE: Always say you're sorry.

THE REALITY: Remember the time you took a pack of gum from the supermarket and your mother made you return it and apologize to the manager? Totally mortifying, we know. But sometimes saying you're sorry is the only way to make things right, even in situations when you don't necessarily think that you were wrong. Taking at least some of the responsibility for a stupid argument with a friend is a better alternative than letting it blow out of proportion and possibly ruin your relationship.

THE RULE: Don't take what isn't yours.

THE REALITY: When it comes to best friends, there are some things that belong in the "what's mine is yours and what's yours is mine" category, including tampons, accessories, and Xanax. Other things should be filed under "not on your life," like significant others (which should go without saying), signature fragrances, and money.

THE RULE: Never talk to strangers.

THE REALITY: Despite your parents' warnings about the creepy guy who drove the blue windowless van (perfect for kidnapping little girls), an unfamiliar face isn't necessarily an unfriendly one. In fact, according to some ancient forms of wisdom (okay, a fortune cookie) strangers are just friends you haven't met yet. So the next time you're standing in an impossibly long line at Starbucks or flipping through a four-month-old copy of a magazine in the waiting room at the gynecologist, strike up a conversation with the equally impatient girl sitting next to you.

THE RULE: Hold hands and stick together.

THE REALITY: Designed to make sure the bus didn't leave without you on the class trip to the museum, the buddy system was, at most, a safety precaution. While it's still a good idea to use it on those nights when you've had one to many and can't be trusted to use your best judgment (or any judgment, for that matter), its purpose has shifted to fulfill a more emotional need. It's a big, scary world out there and we need our friends to support us during the tough times and to cheer for us when things are going well. Knowing that there is someone standing by your side through the good and the bad just makes life easier and a hell of a lot more fun.

THE RULE: Wait your turn.

THE REALITY: Back when you considered Elmer's glue a delicacy, "wait your turn" was a phrase that your mother repeated ad nauseum when she foolishly assumed that you and your sister could share a Pogo Ball. But the older you get and the more your friends' lives seem to advance while your own life remains stuck in neutral, this classroom commandment becomes a personal mantra that you use to remind yourself that your time will come too. The next time something really big happens to one of your friends and you feel happy for them but not as happy as you should, look at it this way: life's a journey, not a destination, and why do all of Aerosmith's songs after 1990 sound exactly the same?

THE RULE: Treat others as you would like to be treated.

THE REALITY: This is the biggie—the golden rule. When it comes to your friends (and everyone, really), you should treat them how you would like them to treat you, unless, of course, you happen to be a masochist. In that case, treat others the exact opposite of how you would like to be treated. Although if the other person is also a masochist, then we guess you should treat her like you want to be treated. Christ on horseback, this is getting too complicated. Okay, to sum it all up: clean up your messes and be a decent person. End of story.

in closing

WHY FRIENDS ARE JUST AS IMPORTANT AS BOYFRIENDS

Guys communicate through a series of grunts while playing Nintendo Wii tennis, whereas women can be a bit high maintenance, or at least overanalytical, when it comes to friendship. But regardless of gender, there's bound to be a little friction among groups of people who really care about one another. (Don't even get us started on family functions.) All of the time, effort, and occasional drama is worth it, because there's nothing quite like the bond between girlfriends. They're your support system, your cheering section, and you don't know what you'd do without them. If you still need some more convincing *(really?)*, here are more reasons why you need your girlfriends:

- Because if Mariah Carey had friends (anyone on the payroll doesn't count) they would introduce her to a fabric that's not Lycra.
- Because your family is required to like you, but your friends hang out with you by choice.
- Because they've heard you tell the same story 183 times but listen to it like it's the first time, every time (or at least pretend to).

- Because only a friend can understand why you order a Diet Coke with your double cheeseburger and fries.
- Because a friend will tell you if the picture on your online dating profile makes you look a little busted.
- Because we're probably going to outlive all of the men, so we need someone to have Rascal races with at the old-folks home.
- Because your cat doesn't understand the nuances of a so-bad-it's-good Lifetime movie starring Tori Spelling, who becomes an escort to help "work her way through school."
- Because you have the best time doing absolutely nothing together.
- Because only a friend has the patience to sit in the dressing room while you try on twenty pairs of jeans and is observant enough to notice which fit the best.
- Because no woman is an island.
- Because your boyfriend can't be your only friend.
- Because life wouldn't be as fun without them.
- Because we're human and part of being human is the need to love and be loved.

Now let's get together and do some trust falls.